Versatile Vernon Kilns

An Illustrated Value Guide
Book II

By Maxine Feek Nelson

COLLECTOR BOOKS
P.O. Box 3009
Paducah, KY 42001

The current values in this book should be used only as a guide. They are not intended to set prices, which vary from one section of the country to another. Auction prices as well as dealer prices vary greatly and are affected by condition as well as demand. Neither the Author nor the Publisher assumes responsibility for any losses that might be incurred as a result of consulting this guide.

Additional copies of this book may be ordered from:

COLLECTOR BOOKS
P.O. Box 3009
Paducah, Kentucky 42001

@ $9.95 Add $1.00 for postage and handling.

Copyright: Maxine Nelson, 1983
ISBN: 0-89145-191-9

This book or any part thereof may not be reproduced without the written consent of the Author and Publisher.

Printed by IMAGE GRAPHICS, Paducah, Kentucky

This book is dedicated to all the people directly or indirec
connected with Vernon Kilns who were instrumental in creati
one of America's outstanding potteries.

ACKNOWLEDGEMENTS

The Nelson residence has been a veritable pottery warehouse for the past several months. Examples of Vernon Kilns to be photographed poured in from collectors and dealers everywhere. My thanks to one and all who have most patiently entrusted me with their favorites, many being rarities.

First I want to credit those whose help made this book possible. To Jack Chipman, who spent two precious commodities, time and gas, driving many 70-mile round trips to lend his talent for art direction at the photo studio and gave me editorial support, my heartfelt thanks. Al Albert, too, deserves special thanks for driving 400 miles to deliver a "truckload" of Vernon pottery to be photographed and for many long-distance calls advising me of new finds. To artist Chuck Steers, for his hours spent producing superb mark renderings and to photographer "Mac" MacClanahan, for many hours and genuine interest, my grateful thanks to both. To David R. Smith, Disney Archivist, my appreciation for his cooperation in sharing heretofore unpublished Disney information. Thanks also to Zepha Bogert, former Vernon Kilns Advertising Manager, who made available company catalogs; to Jane Bennison Howell, daughter of the founder of Vernon Kilns, for sharing her recollections; and to Evelyn Venable Mohr who made a special phone call to provide information about "her" figurine. To Susan Pickell-Hedrick and Virginia Scott, thank you for sharing details of research. To the many who loaned their pottery and shared information, especially Bess Christensen, Joyce and Vic Cochrane, Ruth and Vernon Danison, John and Ann DeMelio, Barbara Erickson, Pat Faux, Kay Hammer, Gerald Harrington, Ron Hillman of The Attic, Sharon Jarrell, Kelly Kalin, Mary Klarich, David and Glenda Laird, Josephine Morse, James Pasquali, Steve Pepper, Mr. Rupert of Pasadena, the proprietors of the Santa Monica Trading Company, Nancy and Bill Schadeberg, Nancy Sessions, Julie Sferrazza, Randy Simon, Trey Springer, Gloria Samario of Gloria's Potpourri, Keith Schneider of Gasoline Alley, Donna Summers, Carol Thomas, J.C. Urcia, Jr., Lois Vacher, Fran and Peter Van Rossem, Mr. and Mrs. Van Fryman, Pat Van Sant, Betty Wanser, Perry Wendt, Margaret and Fred Wilhelm and Jack Chipman and Judy Stangler of California Spectrum, THANK YOU, one and all.

I would like to express appreciation for the Vernon story as told to me by the late Faye G. Bennison, founder and president of Vernon Kilns; to Edward Fischer, its last president; James Cox, former employee; Doug Bothwell, son-in-law of Faye Bennison and to members of the Poxon family and others who filled in the gaps. A word in memoriam for the late John F. Gorton, husband of Sally Kent Gorton (Kent's widow) who was Director of the Rockwell Kent Legacies until his untimely passing in February 1980. Thanks also to Sally and George Spector, Editor of the *Rockwell Kent Newsletter*. And lastly to publisher, Bill Schroeder, gratitude for his faith in my ability to present the story of Vernon Kilns.

PREFACE

It seems like only yesterday, but in reality it was 1946 just after World War II had finally ended, and my husband and I were newlyweds arriving in Southern California. One of our first gifts was a starter set of Vernon's Brown Eyed Susan, sent by my family in Seattle and purchased there at Frederick & Nelson's (Marshall Field's Seattle store). Looking back, I was completely oblivious to the fact that the pottery had been made nearby in the industrial city of Vernon, which bordered south central Los Angeles. However, the day came when this proximity and the pottery itself led to my intensive research into Vernon Kilns.

Meanwhile, twelve years went by and my open stock Susan pattern was suddenly no longer available. Sadly, I learned that the company was out of business so what was left of my set was simply packed away for the time being and forgotten. In the early 1960's I caught the collecting "bug" and would occasionally spot a piece of my old pattern at our local flea markets, noting also an abundance of Vernon Kilns picture plates which were all very inexpensive. Before long I had managed to accumulate quite a collection of the picture plates, including my home state of Washington, Seattle and the University of Washington. Definitely a high point was the day I found a Timothy Mouse figurine at a Los Angeles antique show and was surprised to see it marked "Vernon Kilns" along with the Walt Disney copyright and date.

The purchase of a *Momento* plate signed by Faye G. Bennison, founder and president of Vernon Kilns, ultimately led me on October 13, 1971, to my first visit with this grand old man. At this time I learned firsthand the story of his company and its predecessor, Poxon China. My memory of our last visit will always remain vivid. The late Mr. Bennison was at that time in his 90's, yet remarkably alert. He ushered me into the kitchen of his spacious home, mounted a stepladder and reached the top shelf of a cupboard. Taking down piece by piece, he proudly showed me a complete dinnerware service for twelve in Rockwell Kent's "Salamina" including egg cups, tumblers and serving pieces.

In 1978 my book *Versatile Vernon Kilns* (now out of print) was published. It documented the history of Vernon Kilns and Poxon and all their wares which were known at the time. Since then much more information has surfaced regarding Vernon's versatility; and as the pieces fell into place, the need for a second book with special emphasis on dinnerware became apparent.

Values in this price guide are averages, based upon prices observed in leading national trade publications and those seen in California shops and pottery shows among dealers who specialize in pottery. The prices are for pieces in their original condition, having no wear, chips, cracks, scratches or defective glazes. This is meant to serve as a guide only. Prices will vary from area to area and will be determined by popularity and availability.

TABLE OF CONTENTS

INTRODUCTION

In the early depression years of the 1930's there were many potteries in Southern California busily producing colorful, inexpensive pottery. The region had long been a mecca for artists from all over the world. Many of these talented artists were at work designing and decorating the popular production ware which became a kind of soothing panacea during those hard times.

Vernon Kilns was among these potteries and a successor to an earlier company, Poxon China, which traced its roots to the Gold Rush 49'ers. Poxon China (known also as Vernon China) was founded in Vernon, California about 1912. In 1931 it was sold to Faye G. Bennison and renamed Vernon Kilns (also known as Vernon Potteries, Ltd.).

The company ultimately became a leader in the pottery industry and famous internationally for the quality and versatility of its wares. These included movie star figures, Walt Disney-designed figurines, vases and dinnerware, as well as Coca Cola and other advertising items. Political, fraternal, religious, patriotic, and famous people and places were subjects of the historical and commemorative specialties. Scores of dinnerware patterns were designed by celebrated artists. The pottery was available in better department stores, jewelry and gift stores throughout the United States and Canada with sales offices in all major cities.

Surviving the disasters of a depression, earthquake and fire, and the war years, Vernon Kilns remained one of the country's most successful pottery companies. But like many of its glass and pottery contemporaries, the company was unable to survive the flood of foreign imports, complicated by domestic labor disputes, in the postwar era. In January of 1958 the company reluctantly announced its decision to cease operation and later that year closed its doors forever. Metlox Potteries of Manhattan Beach, California, bought the Vernon tradename, "goodwill", molds and remaining stock, and did continue producing several dinnerware patterns for a very short time (see Dinnerware section). One set of molds for Metlox's own Vernon Ware pottery line is still in use today - none of the patterns are the old Vernon Kilns patterns. However, the majority of Vernon's pottery would never again be produced but was destined to become highly collectible Americana.

EVOLUTION OF MARKS

POXON CHINA marks (also known as Vernon China)

1912-1931:

POXON LOS ANGELES	POXON LOS ANGELES	POXON CHINA VERNON CALIFORNIA	VERNON CHINA VERNON, CAL. 428
(1) 101 Incised	(2) Embossed	(3)	(4)

VERNON KILNS marks (also known as Vernon Potteries, Ltd. - see mark 5)

1930's

(5) Paper label brown & gold Rare!

(6) Mission Bell #1

(7) Sometimes Multicolor

(8) Mission Bell #2-Montecito

VERNON KILNS
CALIFORNIA
MADE IN U.S.A.

(9)

(10) Embossed

(11)

VERNON KILNS
MADE IN U.S.A.
CALIFORNIA

(12)

1930-into early 1940's:

(13)

MODERN
CALIFORNIA
VERNON KILNS
LOS ANGELES
AUTHENTIC
CALIFORNIA POTTERY
MADE IN U.S.A.

(14)

ULTRA CALIFORNIA
VERNON KILNS
AUTHENTIC
CALIFORNIA
POTTERY
MADE IN U.S.A.

(15)

SANTA BARBARA
Designed by
VERNON KILNS
Made in U.S.A.
Pat. Pend. S.E.C.

(16)*

MELINDA
AUTHENTIC
VERNONWARE
VERNON
KILNS
CALIF.
MADE IN U.S.A.

(17)

NATIVE CALIFORNIA
VERNON KILNS
AUTHENTIC
CALIFORNIA
POTTERY
MADE IN U.S.A.

(18)

HAND PAINTED
UNDER GLAZE
VERNON KILNS
CALIF.
MADE IN U.S.A.
Dolores

(19)*

1947:

(20)*

(21)*

(22)

1955:

(23)

VERNON'S
"Tickled Pink"
MADE IN U.S.A.

(24)*

(25)*

(26)*

1956-1960:

(27)*

VERNON WARE
BY
METLOX
MADE IN CALIFORNIA

(28)

Transitional Marks:
(27) also Metlox with added "By Metlox"
(28) Metlox Vernon Ware

*Pattern identity

7

Designer-Artist and Special Marks

JANE F. BENNISON
VERNON KILNS CALIFORNIA
MADE IN U.S.A.

(29)

INLAID GLAZE
Harry Bird
VERNON KILNS
CALIFORNIA
PAT. PEND.
MADE IN U.S.A.

(30)

BIRD POTTERY
VERNON KILNS
CALIFORNIA
MADE IN U.S.A.
PAT. PEND.

(31)

VIEVE HAMILTON POTTERY
MADE IN U.S.A
VERNON KILNS CALIF.
MAY &

(32)

HAND PAINTED UNDER GLAZES
BY
Gale Turnbull
VERNON KILNS
CALIFORNIA

(33)

TASTE
Gale Turnbull
VERNON KILNS
Made in U.S.A.

(34)*

CORAL REEF
Designed by
Aloha
Don Blanding
VERNON KILNS
Made in U.S.A.

(35)*

"OUR AMERICA"
Designed by
Rockwell Kent
VERNON KILNS
Made in U.S.A.

(36)*

NUTCRACKER
Designed by
Walt Disney
Copyright 1940
Vernon Kilns
Made in U.S.A.

(37)*

DISNEY
COPYRIGHT 1940
VERNON KILNS
U.S.A.

(38)-Bisque base

Designed by
WALT DISNEY
Copyright 1940
VERNON KILNS
Made in U.S.A.

(39)

VERNON'S 1860
HAND PAINTED UNDER GLAZE
BY
VERNON KILNS
CALIFORNIA U.S.A.

(40)

MOJAVE
MADE IN
California

(41)

Winchester 73
Hand Painted Under Glaze
By
Vernon Kilns
U.S.A.

(42)

Hand Painted Under Glaze
Frontier Days
BY
VERNON KILNS - CALIFORNIA U.S.A.

(43)

Panamerican Lei
By
Vernon Kilns
CALIFORNIA-U.S.A.

(44)

U.S. MAIL **RFD**
by
Vernon Kilns
California U.S.A.

(45)

HAND PAINTED UNDER GLAZE
Vernon Kilns
Sun Garden
By
Jean Ames
MADE IN CALIFORNIA U.S.A.

(46)

Chatelaine
Sharon Merrill Design - incised
a
Vernonware
California USA
Jade - stamped

(47)

vernon ware
Imperial
made in california

(48)

Note: Marks were underglaze and usually in the color of the predominant pattern
color.
*Pattern identity

8

POXON CHINA (VERNON CHINA)
1912-1931

In 1912 George Poxon (1887-1950) founded the Poxon China Company at 2310 East 52nd Street in Vernon, California, an industrial city on the southern fringe of Los Angeles. A small factory, with two large beehive kilns and one small gloss kiln, was built upon ranch land leased from the prominent Robert Furlong family and adjacent to their ranch house. George Poxon, an honor graduate from Staffordshire Technical College, England, had come to America around 1911 with his uncle William Wade (a member of the Wade pottery family). Not much is known of their path across our country to California, but it is surmised that they journeyed through Ohio because in George Poxon's journal (loaned to the writer by the family) mention is made of several Ohio pottery companies.

In 1913 George married Judith Furlong, youngest daughter of the Robert Furlong children. Mr. Furlong had migrated to California from Ireland during the Gold Rush days to seek his fortune, eventually settling with his family in Southern California. The Furlongs were influential in shaping the future of the city of Vernon as a major western industrial center and are still active in Vernon's city government today.

The new Poxon Company imported workers from George's native England and many came from East Liverpool, Ohio. Eventually a work force existed of around sixty-five employees, including a number of Mexican girls employed in certain phases of production. Very little information is available about the early days of the factory except that they used native California clay from nearby Alberhill. According to former employee James Cox, the methods and equipment were primitive compared to the later days and were much the same as had been used in England. The kilns were heated with gas. The two large ones (14 ft. high by 15 ft. in diameter) took about a day and a half to heat and the small one only about a day.

The first Poxon products were small hexagonal-shaped tiles, the type used on bathroom floors. Some art pottery was also made, such as the El Camino Real 10″ vase decorated with a lamp post and mission bell. One of these is reported to be housed in the Smithsonian Institution in Washington, D.C.

George's specialty was glazing, and a good example of this is seen in the picture of Poxon art pottery on page 10. The smaller bowl on the left in the picture is believed to be a salesman's sample.

At the onset of World War I the company shifted to producing earthenware dishes and heavy hotel and restaurant-type ware. A few plates were handpainted. European decals, popular with all the American chinaware manufacturers, were mostly used. Sometime during this period the company also used the name "Vernon China". The same dish patterns might be marked either Poxon China or Vernon China, marks 3 and 4 respectively, as illustrated in Evolution of Marks section.

The figural bell, undoubtedly a symbol of the California missions, is believed to have been a dealer sign for Poxon's Vernon China line. The "Mission Bell" symbol was later adopted by Poxon's successor, Vernon Kilns, as one of its first trademarks. When the Great Depression hit and hard times befell the Poxon Company, the family decided to sell out and in 1931 the company was bought by Faye G. Bennison.

George Poxon went on to organize the Electric Tile Company in Whittier, California. Later he joined Wallace China on Soto Street in Los Angeles, according to the family. It is believed he was also associated with Catalina Clay Products, located on

Catalina Island off the coast of Southern California. In his last years, George worked as a chemist at Trona, California, for a borax company where he also held a mining claim which produced raw material for a distinctive red glaze. Here he also researched and taught pottery making and his first love, glazing. George Poxon died of leukemia in 1950. His wife, Judith, passed away in 1967 in Vernon in the ranch house where she had spent her entire life.

Today nothing remains of the original ranch. The large buildings which now stand on the site of the first factory were built by Vernon Kilns and, at last report, are now occupied by a carpet firm.

Identifying pottery marks are numbered in parentheses or marked with a "U" for unmarked. See Evolution of Marks section for sequence of mark numbers.

Examples of Poxon art pottery, all scarce.

Left to right: 4½″ dark blue bowl (2), has intact paper label on bottom which reads "Shape #1, Size 4, Original price $6.00, Color C". Brown clay is highlighted under the glaze, $35.00; 10″ bowl No. 101 with interesting glaze (1), $65.00. George Poxon's specialty was glazing. Another bowl, No. 103 with dark brown and green glaze, is known and has an incised script "Poxon, Los Angeles" mark; El Camino Real 10″ vase, hexagonal sided (1), stoneware bisque finish, high glaze light green interior, $100.00. The embossed design represents the light standards that once dotted California's El Camino Real - "The Kings Highway" - and the mission bell represents the chain of 21 missions linked by the early Highway. (The first missions appeared in the late 1700's and were built from adobe by Indians under the direction of Franciscan missionaries led by Father Junipero Serra.) A few of the light standards are standing still along today's modern El Camino Real.

13″ game plate, decal, artist signed R.K. Becker (4), $45.00.

9½″ handpainted peacock plate (3), $25.00.

Poxon/Vernon China dishes utilizing decals. All have mark 4 unless noted.

Top, left to right: Child's mug, $12.00; 9″ plate, $8.00; gravy boat, $7.50; 9½″ plate (3), $5.00. Center, left to right: Two children's mugs, $12.00; hotel-type mug (3), $4.00; 7″ soup, $10.00; 9″ oval vegetable bowl, $7.50. Bottom, left to right: 4½″ purple bell, embossed "Vernon China", dealer sign, $35.00.

THE FOUNDING OF VERNON KILNS (VERNON POTTERIES, LTD.) 1931

Poxon China set the stage for Vernon Kilns, founded by Faye G. Bennison. Mr. Bennison in his privately published "Our Family" history said, "Some people seem to have little curiosity or a desire to know from whence they came, but I do believe that the vast majority of this family will not only be interested but will carry on the family records for generations to come." Vernon Kilns pictorial pottery is further evidence of his belief in documenting American historical events, people and places for future generations of American people.

Born in Creston, Iowa, on March 6, 1883, Faye Bennison learned merchandising early from his hardworking father who owned a small chain of prosperous mercantile stores. Educated at Morgan Park Academy in Illinois and the Bond Institute of Mercantile Training in New York City*, Mr. Bennison opened a dry goods store in Cedar Falls in 1908. When hard times hit the Iowa farmlands, he sold the store and in 1921 moved his family - a wife and three small daughters - to California. In California he invested in a glass factory that made bottles and jars, going in as Secretary-Treasurer and eventually became General Manager and Vice-President. This company flourished and was bought by Owens-Illinois Glass. It was at this time that Mr. Bennison crossed paths with the Poxons who were looking for a buyer for their pottery. In July 1931 he acquired the company, became President and General Manager and in his words "immediately changed the name to Vernon Kilns".

The former owners maintained a lively interest in the company which remained on their ranch land. As part of the mortgage agreement, members of the Poxon and Furlong families were promised two complete dinnerware sets of their choosing every year for as long as they desired.

Despite prevailing economic depression, Mr. Bennison instigated major changes upon assuming ownership of the pottery. Between eighty-five and one hundred competent people were hired including some employees of the former company. Edward J. Fischer, an accountant for Poxon, joined the new company and remaind loyal to "the boss" even after the doors of the pottery were closed. As told by James Cox, a former Poxon employee who stayed on as kiln man, "Mr. Bennison came in during the bad years, the depression, yet he saw that nobody earned less than $10.00 a week and kept our morale high. He told us to go along with him and we'd come out of this 'maybe not eating steak, but you'll be eating'."

For awhile the company continued with remaining Poxon stock, producing a variety of decaled ware. The Mexican motif - reported to have been premium ware in sacks of tortilla flour - is an example. The Poxon blanks were fairly heavy and the shapes had embossed and scalloped rims. A variety of patterns, including the Mexican motif and the Autumn Leaf decal, are pictured and described. Though no doubt scarce, place settings and serving pieces might be found in these early Vernon Kilns patterns utilizing Poxon blanks.

The first Mission Bell mark (6) and the script "Vernon" (7) are the backstamps most often found on the pottery of this early period. Note the monogram "VPL" within the square overlaying the letter "V" of the Vernon mark (7). This probably signified the initials of Vernon Potteries, Ltd., the less commonly used name of Vernon Kilns. In *Versatile Vernon Kilns Book I,* I stated that these marks were believed to be Poxon's, but all evidence now indicates they are the first marks of Vernon Kilns.

An early paper label having gold lettering and mission arch on a dark brown background (5) is rarely found. After fifty years, this label, remarkably intact, has remained affixed to an unusual sugar bowl which was found recently along with some unmarked Early California grill plates at an estate sale in Pennsylvania. Thanks to a Pennsylvania dealer, the sugar bowl is now in the author's collection but arrived too late for photographing. (See dinnerware section for description of sugar bowl.)

It is presumed that the initial period of production ended with the destructive earthquake that hit Southern California in 1933. Most of the pottery stock was shattered as it fell to the concrete floor of the factory. Truckloads of broken pieces had to be hauled away and extensive repairs were made to the beehive kilns. This probably prompted the decision to design new molds. As a result, the disaster was followed by an era of unparalleled success as the company was forced to start afresh.

*At that time the Bond Institute was affiliated with Columbia University where today in the University museum, examples of Vernon's Rockwell Kent china can be found.

These next three photos attempt to show the gradual transition of Vernon Kilns from decals on Poxon shapes to decals on combination of Poxon and Vernon's own shapes and finally the production of decal ware used exclusively on Vernon Kilns shapes.

Vernon Kilns dinnerware, Poxon shapes backstamps indicated.

Top, left to right:
Scenic 9½" plate (7), $8.00; square 9½" plate, Spanish tile illusion (7), $8.50; Cactus decor on cup and saucer and 9½" plate (6) - cup $3.50, saucer $1.50, plate $5.00.

Bottom, left to right:
9" plate (6), handpainted, $3.50; 5½" fruit, $2.50, and 6½" plate, $2.50, both Cactus (6); 9½" scenic plate (7), $8.00.

The cactus was a popular motif with other china manufacturers. Hall China used the same decal in 1937, Limoges Pottery had a similar Posey Shop pattern and Japan did an excellent copy of Cactus.

This shows Vernon's use of the same decals on both Poxon and Vernon Kilns shapes. In this group are two popular motifs: Autumn Leaf and the Mexicana scene. The Mexicana was produced on both Poxon and Vernon's own shapes. All bear mark 6 unless noted.

Top, left to right:
9″ Floral plate, $5.00; saucer with basket of flowers and silver spattered rim (also backstamped "Pure Sterling Silver"), $1.50; 12″ platter (7), $9.00 -- this platter is identical to plate pictured in Poxon dinnerware photo*; 8½″ vegetable bowl, $7.50.

Bottom, left to right:
5½″ fruit, $3.00, 11½″ platter, marked "18 Karat Gold", $12.00, both are the Mexicana pattern on Poxon shape; creamer, $6.00, and sugar, $7.00, both Mexicana on Vernon's Coronado** cubist shape. Creamer and sugar are unmarked except "22 Karat Gold" on the sugar; Vernon's Autumn Leaf 5½″ fruit, Poxon shape (7), $7.50, scarce; 5½″ fruit, color band design, $1.50.

*Mark on this platter substantiates the theory that Vernon Kilns did continue with Poxon stock and patterns.
**Coronado shape is described in the dinnerware section.

Decals on Vernon's original Montecito*, exceptions noted, three pieces bear the Montecito mark 8.

Top, left to right:
9½" plate, dainty floral border (8), $4.50; 5" diameter sugar, floral bouquet (8), $6.00; 9½" plate, scenic (9), $8.00; 8½" plate, floral, matching sugar (8), $3.50.

Center, left to right:
7½" plate, wild rose border (9), $3.50; 6" plate (Not Montecito, but Poxon blank), marked "Nasco, Pure Silver and Platinum decoration"**, (6) $3.00; 10" oval vegetable, wild rose border (9), $7.50; 9" round vegetable, floral on yellow background (13), $7.50.

Bottom, left to right:
Wild rose creamer (U) $4.00, cup (U) $3.00, and saucer (9) $1.00; sauce boat, hand-painted bands (10), $3.50.

*Montecito shape is described in the dinnerware section.
**This indicates some dinnerware was jobbed since Nasco is a name often found on Japanese ware. Another dinnerware pattern has been found having Vernon's mark 9 and "Pacific China Company" executed on the Montecito shape.

16

ART WARE

In the mid-thirties, the company established an artware department which was a brief departure from their dinnerware and specialty ware.

Jane Bennison, the talented daughter of the owner, worked summers from 1931 to 1935 while a student at the University of Southern California. After obtaining her art degree, she joined the company as a full-fledged artist and stayed on for two years creating many pottery vases, bowls, candlesticks and figurines. She was also responsible for the design of the distinctive "upside-down" handles applied to the Ultra holloware (which was a Gale Turnbull design). Her personal trademark was an anchor riding the waves (29), the anchor being her college sorority insignia.

About the same time another artist, Harry Bird, was associated with Vernon Kilns. Little is known of the man but according to Jane Bennison, he had arranged with the company to use its facilities and decorate dinnerware with his own designs. His was a unique (patented) method of applying colored glaze. To form the design he used a silver-tipped syringe achieving an embossed effect and afterwards, firing again with a clear satiny glaze. This process was sometimes designated "Inlaid Glaze." In 1937 two ads for Vernon pottery featured designs by Harry Bird. One pictured Spectrum, a series of geometric designs, each in a different combination of colors, described as a "new design by famed artist Harry Bird . . . an exclusive Vernon creation - the bright glaze is inlaid-handwork." The specific colors were not mentioned in the ad. The other ad pictured movie star Delores Del Rio holding a piece of Vernon pottery, Olinala Ware. The ware was a re-creation of authentic Aztec designs and according to the ad, "old when found by Cortez, Miss Del Rio rediscovered the Aztec ware and commissioned Harry Bird to re-create it in faithful reproduction . . ." The ad also states that the designs were soft blue, green, yellow or rose on a warm background. All Harry Bird ware is scarce but Olinala is especially rare. The Olinala plate pictured belongs to a former employee of the factory and is one of the only two pieces the writer has seen.

Harry Bird's personal trademark depicted his name in script signature (30) or a "bird" (31) over the name Vernon Kilns. Prior to joining Vernon, Bird is believed to have had his own pottery studio in Pasadena, California. He used Vernon Kilns blanks but without the trademark of Vernon Kilns, which explains why some Bird decorated pottery is found on Vernon pottery with only the Bird mark. While Harry Bird's Vernon Kilns pottery cannot be classified as strictly "studio" ware, it is definitely unique in artistic style.

Accomplished artists, Diane May Hamilton de Causse and Genevieve Bartlett Hamilton Montgomery, were sisters who worked together at Vernon Kilns. They created a line of vases, figurines, plaques and at least two dinnerware lines, Rhythmic and Rippled. Their pottery was generally produced in solid pastels with a doeskin-like finish. Work was signed with their trademark, a Pekingese dog over the name Vernon Kilns in a circle (32). The Hamilton sisters were said to have complementing personalities, May the calm one and Vieve the fiesty of the two. May was reported to have been married to de Causse, the designer of the Franklin car, but, in later years, the sisters lived together in Pasadena, virtually penniless. During their careers, they were listed in *Who's Who in American Art*.

Jane Bennison and Harry Bird shared the desire to continue the art line but it was ruled out about 1937 due to the economic situation.

Jane Bennison 12″ Art Deco Bust, fine example of the creative style of the 1930 period, (29), $150.00 (scarce).

Jane Bennison Art Line. All items bear the "anchor" backstamp (29). These were made in various colors and as many as six different numbered sizes.

Top, left to right:
Moon bowl No. 1, 7½" high, $30.00; 12" console bowl (backstamped Salad Bowl #1), $35.00; pair of 4½" hexagonal candlesticks (matching hexagonal shaped bowl is known), $35.00; fluted 10" pedestal bowl, $35.00. Rockwell Kent's Moby Dick in blue has been found decorating this piece.

Bottom, left to right:
Dayrae No. 3, 11½" bowl which came in a wide range of colors, $25.00 (Dayrae No. 1 measures 15½" and was used for Rockwell Kent's Moby Dick line in orange); Rectangular bowl, 10" x 4" (not numbered but other sizes have been reported) $35.00; Pine Cone No. 2, 5½" bowl, $35.00; 11" Walnut bowl features embossed walnut halves around outside rim and a walnut shell handle, $45.00.

Other items reported but not pictured include spherical candlesticks, a tripod candlestick, and a hand-decorated Phoenix bird open back planter, measuring 18" long and 10" high.

Pictured at right are florals and geometrics by Harry Bird. All are executed on the Montecito shape and bear the Bird mark except where noted.

Top, left to right:
Multi Flori California Green 9½" plate, $12.00; Multi Flori California Brown 6½" plate, $6.50, also marked "Made Expressly for Barker Bros." (An old and well known Los Angeles furniture store). In Multi Flori, the colors are monocromatic as indicated in the pattern name. Additional colors are blue, yellow and rose. B-327 7½" plate, $7.50; B-327 1 quart pitcher (30), $18.00. B-327 is an identical pattern to Multi Flori except the colors are polychromatic. Both Multi Flori and B-327 may be of the **Spectrum** series.

2nd row, left to right:
Morning Glory*; Bird's Eye*; Mariposa Tulip*; each 10½" plates, $25.00 each.

3rd row, left to right:
Desert Mallow*; B-156 (31); Phacelia*; each 10½" plates, $25.00 each.

Bottom, left to right:
Phacelia* teapot, $45.00; Olinala-Aztec, Blue on Satin 10½" plate, $30.00; 9½" plate* (not named), $12.00; Evening Star blue and ivory demitasse cup (one of Bird's solid color group), $10.00; BB-2 creamer, $10.00, and sugar, $15.00 (all are marked 31). The letter "B" no doubt indicates a Bird design.

Other Harry Bird patterns known are: Vert*, Beige (solid color), Golden Maple (solid color), Polychrome A, Tahiti C* and Petunia.
A partial set of Bird dinnerware consisting of a mixed group of florals and "Tropical Fish" (identical to "Fish" pictured) has been found. Some of the same florals already mentioned above plus the patterns Iris, Geranium, Wild Pink, Trumpet Flower, Golden Brodiaea, Water Lily and Columbine decorate the ware in Bird's typical glaze underglaze on ivory satin background, executed on Montecito shape. Two other Montecito items also in the set are a 5½" dish with applied center handle (probably intended as a lemon server) and a 3-part oval relish, 10" x 7½". All carry the Bird mark 31 and pattern name without the Vernon Kilns tradename, except for one piece which does have the Vernon Kilns name.

*These items do not have Vernon Kiln's name on the backstamp.

Harry Bird Pottery. What a delight to possess a dinnerware set in any of these vibrantly colored patterns, mixed or matched! Animals, fish and solids all executed on Vernon's Montecito, exceptions noted.

Top, left to right:
Pomegranate 16″ platter (31), $35.00; After Glow 14″ chop plate (30), $25.00.
Bottom, left to right:
Pig* 15″ bowl decorated with figures of rabbit, swan, fawn and pig (maybe Poxon shape), $65.00; colorful tropical Fish* 13″ bowl, $55.00; B-310 chowder bowl of the **Spectrum** series (31), $12.00; Fish* cup matching Fish bowl (marked only "Bird Pottery, Patent Pend."), $15.00.

Close-up of rare Olina-Aztec, Blue on Satin, $25.00.

*Backstamp does not include Vernon Kilns name.

22

May and Vieve Hamilton Art Line. Each was made in different colors and some came in several sizes. All have the Hamilton mark (32).

Milady Vase, 7½", ivory high glaze, $30.00 (there are companion pieces, a Milady Bowl No. 2, 12" x 6" flat rectangular with embossed bow design in center, and bowshaped candleholders); 12" tray, engraved abstract leaf and ruffled flower petal in center, pale aqua satin finish, $40.00; Cylinder No. 3, 8" aqua vase, $25.00 (three sizes are known, No. 1 the largest); Godey Lady, 10" period costumed figure, ivory color, hollow base, $75.00; Rose Bowl No. 4, 5" aqua satin finish, has four narrow concentric rings on upper shoulder and neck, $25.00; Pierced Plate, striking 16½" plaque, reticulated 4½" rim and engraved abstract design of nude female and palm tree, $85.00; stately yellow bird, 7½", tail forms tray, $45.00.

Also known are Spheres, a bowl similar to Rose Bowl, Cosmic 13" diameter bowl, 6½" deep, sloped sides to 4" diameter, ringed 1" deep footed base, and Calas No. 3 lily-shaped vase.

Rhythmic and Rippled dinnerware by the Hamiltons. All bear mark (32) except where noted. The Rippled pattern has graduated narrow rings on rim and known colors are pink, lemon yellow, ivory, lavender and bright blue. The Rhythmic design has three exactly-spaced stepped down rings and known colors are yellow, pink, blue and ivory. Holloware items in Rhythmic are rounded compared to the geometric Rippled shape.

Rippled 7″ lug chowder, $12.00; Rippled cup, $12.00 and saucer, $3.00; Rippled 10½″ pink plate, $15.00; Rhythmic plates, sizes 9½″, $10.00, 7½″, $7.50, and 6½″, $5.00 (the 9½″ ivory plate has greenish undertones and is the only unmarked piece); 4-cup teapot (note down turn to handles), $40.00.

FAMOUS ARTIST-DESIGNERS

Gale Turnbull

There was an overlap in the "art" pottery period and the hiring of Gale Turnbull as Art Director in 1936. Gale Turnbull, painter and engraver, had already achieved recognition for his designs at Leigh Potteries of Alliance, Ohio, in 1930 and later at Sebring Pottery. His credits included a listing in *Who's Who in American Art*, membership in the American Art Association of Paris, France, and his works were exhibited in the Museum of Modern Art in Paris and the Brooklyn Museum in New York.

The renowned and highly respected Frederick Rhead in his "Art and Design Committee Report" to the 55th Annual Convention of the U.S. Potters Association in 1933 said, "The acquisition by the tableware manufacturers . . . of men such as Gale Turnbull, Joseph Thorley and Victor Schreckengost has already resulted in development activities which have raised the standards of tableware design and by examples exercised favorable influence over those concerns who do not yet employ art specialists." In his report at the 56th Annual Convention in December 1934, he said "Gale Turnbull is the first ceramic artist in the American tableware game to emphasize the beauty of color in tableware decoration." And again at the 58th Annual Convention in December 1936 he reported "The Vernon Potteries of California, who within the past year (1936) acquired Gale Turnbull have produced some interesting printed and filled-in [hand-tinted ware], and also some handpainted underglaze craft types, of a Continental flavor Both shapes and decorations are fundamentally sound, and the potting is among the best we have seen in semi-vitreous practice."

Vernon Kilns, a pacesetter, with Gale Turnbull as Art Director, hired celebrated artists who were given the freedom to create their best in their own studios in various parts of the country, with Mr. Turnbull traveling to supervise. Again, Frederick Rhead in his 60th Annual Convention report of January 1939 stated, "One of our group, Vernon Potteries of Los Angeles, has made a most interesting experiment in this direction (underglaze printing). With Gale Turnbull as Art Director they turn up at this year's Pittsburgh Show with two tableware decorations by Rockwell Kent and two more by Don Blanding. Three of the patterns are underglaze prints in one color, the fourth, also underglaze, is in outline and beautifully hand-tinted by well-trained art students." He went on to report "It is enough to state without any reservation that it is the greatest and most inspiring development since the production of Wedgewood's Queensware and the old Staffordshire underglaze prints. It is so far above anything that has been done in any country by any potter since that time that comparison would be idiotic. Anyone at present in the tableware business who fails to appreciate or to recognize the significance of this development is in that class of potters whose organization have ceased to exist for no other reason than that they starved themselves to death for lack of creative vision."

And finally in his Committee report at the 61st Annual Convention of the U.S. Potters Association in January 1940 he commented, "The Rockwell Kent American series cannot be ignored, it is another advance in the history of American ceramic creative development. With proper care and attention to marketing, the Rockwell Kent and Don Blanding decorations will last for generations." In essence these few words of Frederick Rhead echo the thought expressed by Faye Bennison in his "Our Family" and evidenced in the pottery of Vernon Kilns. Rhead's recognition of Turnbull's talent and the importance of his acquisition as head of the Art Department are evidence too of Faye Bennison's outstanding leadership and farsightedness.

During his years with Vernon, Turnbull's output of designs was abundant. He is credited with the Ultra shape and many handpainted as well as printed and hand-tinted designs as pictured in the Dinnerware section of this book. Marks 33 or 34 were used on Turnbull designs, sometimes only his initials as part of the mark. It is not known for certain when Turnbull left Vernon but probably in the early 1940's. However, his creative influence remained for the duration of the company.

A Zodiac series (no doubt there are 12) was handpainted by Gale Turnbull. Too late for photographing, one of these has been found which pictures a lion standing and the zodiac sign and is executed on a Montecito 10½" plate. The backstamp includes Turnbull's mark and the identifying words "Zodiac, Leo". The artwork is unmistakably Turnbull's.

Don Blanding

Under Gale Turnbull's supervision, Don Blanding (1894-1957) was the first of the famous artists to design and add his signature to pieces of Vernon Kilns dinnerware. Known as the "Hawaiian poet," he was a globe-trotter, author, and lecturer as well as an artist and illustrator. His travels took him to the tropics where he worked and lived among the Hawaiians, writing and illustrating many delightful books of poetry, such as *Hula Moons, Leaves from a Grass House,* and *Vagabond House* - all collector items today.

While associated with Vernon, Don Blanding worked from his studio in Carmel-by-the-Sea, California and lived at Vagabond House, an old rambling redwood inn which is still standing. It has been said that the proprietor will eagerly point out the room where Blanding lived.

He created four basic tropical designs, two that were floral and two that were fish. Identical designs in different colors were often given a different pattern name, for a total of ten known patterns on the Ultra shape. His Lei Lani, one of the most popular Vernon Kilns patterns of all time, appeared in 1939 magazine ads and was still available by special order as late as June 1955. In 1942 Lei Lani was, for a short time, executed on the Melinda shape and called Hawaii. By 1947 the San Marino shape had been designed and production of Lei Lani was continued on it. His patterns were almost always marked "Aloha, Don Blanding" in signature with the Vernon Kilns name, though sometimes the pattern name was not included. (35)

Rockwell Kent

In the late 1930's Mr. Bennison went to New York to contact Rockwell Kent (1882-1971), a celebrated painter, author, lecturer and illustrator. He hired him to design dinnerware patterns which are now museum pieces. An artist of the social realist school, Kent illustrated everything from large-scale public works murals, greeting cards, magazine ads, book plates, and record album covers to dinnerware. The Kent dinnerware is considered by Kentiana collectors to be the scarcest of all. Kent, who became a controversial figure during the McCarthy investigations of the 1950's, is today honored as one of America's outstanding artists of the twentieth century.

Between 1938 and 1940, Kent, working in his New York studio, designed pictorials which were to decorate three dinnerware patterns: Salamina, Moby Dick and Our America. Each piece would have Rockwell Kent's signature (36) over the Vernon Kilns name. All the Kent patterns were transfer-print designs, Salamina requiring some tinting. The Kent dinnerware unfortunately was way ahead of its time and although major stores throughout the country placed large orders, about half was returned since it did not sell. Consequently, production was discontinued and not too much is found. Kent was unhappy and blamed the "upside down" handles of the Ultra California shape. However, contrary to his criticism, the handles were functional and comfortable and the pitchers did pour.

In 1929 Kent visited Greenland and in 1931 returned again for a year's stay. He later wrote and illustrated the book *Salamina*, named for his faithful housekeeper in Greenland. The colorful Salamina dinnerware pictures her among the icebergs of the Arctic Circle and the flaming rainbows of the Northern landscape. The company brochure described it: "Beautiful enough for the wall of an art museum", and it truly is!

For Our America, Kent drew over thirty different designs illustrating scenes and activities typical of the various regions of the United States. Moby Dick features whaling scenes from Kent's illustrations for the Herman Melville classic. It was the most popular of the Kent dinnerware. A Vernon Kilns 12-piece place setting of Moby Dick in walnut brown is housed at Columbia University in Special Collections, a gift of Kent's widow, Sally Kent Gorton. Further detail about the Kent ware is outlined in the Dinnerware Section.

Both Kent and Blanding plates and bowls are sometimes found in Farber Bros. metal display rims. Farber Bros. of New York City - **not** Farberware -bought the ware from Vernon Kilns and sold the finished product. During World War II the metal transfer plates of all the Rockwell Kent designs were melted down for the zinc and copper necessary for defense production.

Today there is an international group of Rockwell Kent collectors. Several hundred subscribe to "The Kent Collector", a quarterly publication by George Spector of New York (34-10-94th Street, Jackson Heights, N.Y. 11372). This fascinating publication first issued in 1974 contains a wealth of information. Articles are written by well-known authors and personalities, some of whom knew Kent personally. Also featured are ads wanting and selling Kentiana as well as a calendar of upcoming auctions by major art galleries.

Walt Disney

Vernon Kilns signed a contract on October 10, 1940 with the famous Walt Disney Productions to make figures of the characters from the animated film classics *Fantasia, Dumbo* and *The Reluctant Dragon*. During the contract years (1940-1941), vases and tableware were also produced using various Fantasia designs.

Fantasia is the animated film production that gains in popularity and prestige the more aged it becomes. During production -over four years at Disney Studios in Burbank- -many of the thousand or so people involved in the various aspects of *Fantasia's* production felt it was too daring and experimental for Disney. Unfortunately the 1940 public was not ready for such a concept and stayed away from the film even though the critics agreed it was well worth viewing. Disney was disappointed and felt it was a commercial failure - his judgement remained unchanged for the rest of his life. Today it is considered one of the great film classics and is enjoying large audiences at frequent revivals.

The Disney artists attempted to accomplish through eight sequences in *Fantasia*, mental images which occur when listening to classical music. The eight sequences were brought to "life" in cartoon forms against the musical backgrounds of "Toccata and Fugue in D Minor", "The Nutcracker Suite," "The Sorcerer's Apprentice", "Rite of Spring", "The Pastoral Symphony", "Dance of the Hours", "Night on Bald Mountain" and "Ave Maria".

The figurines made by Vernon Kilns were produced from the actual models used in production of the film and are extremely rare. All Vernon figures are believed to be numbered and bear the trademarks "Vernon Kilns, U.S.A.," and "Disney, Copyright 1940" or "1941". This mark is a black-ink stamped block letter mark on the bottom rim (38) and the number of each figurine is impressed in the unglazed underside body. Each high-glaze figure took a minimum of thirty minutes to handpaint and the figures sold for $1.00 to $2.50. Due to high production costs, the figures were discontinued after a short run.

Listed and numbered are all figures known at this time as follows:

2 - 4½ " Satyr	10 - 4½ " Sprite
3 - 4½ " Satyr	11 - 4½ " Sprite
4 - 4½ " Satyr	12 - 4½ " Sprite
5 - 4½ " Satyr	13 - Unicorn, black with yellow horn
6 - 4½ " Sprite	14 - 5 " Unicorn, white
7 - 4½ " Sprite	15 - 6 " Unicorn, white
8 - 3 " reclining Sprite	16 - 5½ " Unicorn, white
9 - 4½ " Satyr	17 - 5½ " reclining Centaurette

18 - 7½" Centaurette
19 - 4½" baby Pegasus, black
20 - 5" Pegasus, white, head turned
21 - 5½" Pegasus, white
22 - 8½" Centaurette
23 - 8" Nubian Centaurette
24 - 7½" Nubian Centaurette
25 - 5" Elephant
26 - Elephant with trunk raised
27 - 5½" Elephant

28 - 6" Ostrich
29 - 8" Ostrich
30 - 9" Ostrich
31 - 10" Centaur
32 - 5½" Hippo
33 - Hippo
34 - 5" Hippo
35 - 3½" Mushroom pepper shaker
36 - 3½" Mushroom salt shaker

Number 1 is the only missing figurine at this writing. It is believed there was an alligator and it might be the missing number. Disney Archives confirms that Vernon Kilns did not make a Fantasia Mickey Mouse.

A pair of 3½" mushroom salt and pepper shakers, numbered 35 and 36 and known as Hop Low were added to the line in June, 1941, and were sold to benefit the United China Relief. These were made by American Pottery.

Vases and bowls also were designed with different motifs from *Fantasia*. The designs are in high relief, and are found in different color combinations, sometimes hand decorated. These are marked "Designed by WALT DISNEY, Copyright 1940" and "VERNON KILNS, Made in U.S.A." (39). The mark was stamped in block letters and numbered under glaze. Sometimes there is also an embossed number. Vases known are as follows:

120 - Mushroom bowl, rectangular, 2" high, 12" x 7"
121 - Goldfish bowl, 6" high, 6" diameter
122 - Winged Nymph bowl, 2½" high, 12" base diameter
123 - Winged Nymph vase, 7" high, 4" diameter
124 - Satyr bowl, 3" high, 6½" diameter
125 - Sprite bowl, 10½" diameter, 3" high
126 - Goddess vase, 10" high, 6½" wide, 4½" across
127 - Pegasus vase, 8" high, 12" wide, 5" across

The *Fantasia* dinnerware patterns were made to complement the figures and vases and were sold in open stock and sets. Patterns were Milkweed Dance, Autumn Ballet, Fairyland, Fantasia (all identical patterns but in different color combinations) Flower Ballet, Enchantment, Dewdrop Fairies and Nutcracker (identical patterns, different color combinations). One other reported pattern called Firefly has not been identified. According to the Disney Archivist, another company had a previous right to use the word "Fantasia" on a set of chinaware. Vernon Kilns apparently made a few sets before they were informed of this fact.

Original retail prices for dinnerware patterns Autumn Ballet, Enchantment, Fairyland, Flower Ballet and Nutcracker were: 14 piece breakfast set - $12.15; 20 piece set - $13.20; 32 piece set - $21.45; 45 piece set - $35.40.

Dewdrop Fairies and Milkweed Dance patterns originally sold for: 14 piece set -$9.15; 20 piece set - $10.00; 32 piece set - $16.45; 45 piece set - $26.90.

Price differences were due to multicolor hand-tint decorating on the first group of patterns above; whereas the second group was a one-color print on an ivory background.

Each piece of dinnerware has the pattern name backstamped in block letters under the glaze along with "designed by Walt Disney" (script signature), copyright date and

"Vernon Kilns, Made in U.S.A." (37). Dinnerware patterns are described and pictured in the Dinnerware section.

Dumbo was typical of Disney's successful animated films and won immediate acclaim. The adorable figurines known to be recreated by Vernon are: 38 - 6″ Timothy Mouse; 40 & 41 - 5″ Dumbo, 2 poses; 42 - 8¾″ Mr. Stork. No. 39 is believed to have been the Crow.

All are dated 1941 and have the Disney copyright and Vernon Kilns, U.S.A. mark (38). Unmarked Dumbo figures identical to Vernon Kilns probably are Evan Shaw's American Pottery figures, although many companies have made these figures. A Dumbo figural planter vase has also been reported but its number is unknown.

Baby Weems, from the full length feature film with animated sequences, *The Reluctant Dragon*, was another Disney figure designed by Vernon Kilns. The 6″ Baby Weems No. 37, dated 1941, has both the Disney and Vernon Kilns trademarks (38).

Extremely rare are personalized Baby Weems made expressly for Mr. Edward J. Fischer, last President of Vernon Kilns, and given to friends to announce the birth of his daughter in 1941. Personalized words appear on the base of each of these.

American Pottery, *Fantasia* and *Dumbo* Figures

Vernon Kilns manufactured and sold Disney designs for only a year and a half. On July 22, 1942, Disney agreed to Vernon Kilns assigning their contract to Evan K. Shaw's American Pottery Company.* Shaw purchased Vernon's stock of figures on hand at that time, along with all the molds, blocks and cases. It was learned from the Disney Archivist that Shaw continued to manufacture the two *Dumbo* designs. Two *Fantasia* figures with American Pottery paper labels have been reported - a hippo and an elephant - as well as the mushroom shakers. For this reason one can conjecture with some certainty that unmarked *Fantasia* or *Dumbo* figures are American Pottery with paper labels missing. The writer has discovered certain distinctions between unmarked and marked figures. Vernon Kilns figures are usually marked with an incised number in the unglazed underside body. American Pottery figures examined have not had any numbers and are glazed inside the body cavity. Further, they tend to be slightly larger than Vernon's and their glaze and handwork sometimes seem to lack some of the quality and detail. For purposes of comparison, in the following photograph, bottom row, the sprite between the two unicorns is unmarked and one can detect the slight difference in size. The elephant in the second photo far left, second row, is also unmarked but is pictured to show the figure in lieu of a marked Vernon example. The two Dumbos are also American Pottery, the one on the far right has the American Pottery label. Again these are shown in lieu of Vernon figures. The writer has compared American Pottery's unmarked Timothy Mouse to Vernon Kilns and again finds Vernon's slightly smaller, better in detail and glaze, and bisque within the body cavity as well as having all the noted markings. However, all are rare and this is not an attempt to discount, only to point out differences.

*Evan K. Shaw acquired Metlox Pottery of Manhattan Beach, California in 1946. He passed away in February, 1980.

Disney figures by Vernon Kilns are adorable and saucy creatures that capture the imagination. It is believed the Vernon Kilns figures were always numbered and marked (38). These are figures from *Fantasia*.

Top, left to right:
Nubian Centaurettes 23 and 24, $200.00; rearing Unicorn 15, $175.00; winged Sprite 10, $75.00.

2nd row, left to right:
Baby black Pegasus 19, $150.00; Centaur 31, $250.00; Centaurette 22, $200.00.

Bottom, left to right:
Satyrs 2 and 5, $75.00; Sprites 7 and 6, $75.00; Donkey Unicorn 16, $175.00; Sprite 11 (unmarked American Pottery, 11 is the Vernon identifying number--note its slightly larger size), $75.00; sitting Unicorn 14, $175.00.

Close-up of *Fantasia* figures.

Donkey Unicorn 16, $175.00; reclining Centaurette 17, $200.00; sitting Unicorn 14, $175.00.

Figures from *Fantasia, Dumbo* and *The Reluctant Dragon.*

Top, left to right: *Fantasia* Ostrich ballerinas 28 and 29, $200.00. 2nd row, left to right: Elephant* (American Pottery, unmarked and not numbered), $125.00; Hippo in Tutu 32, $150.00. Both figures from *Fantasia.* Bottom, left to right: Hop Low mushroom shakers 36, $75.00 pr.; Baby Weems 37, $100.00; Dumbo* wearing clown hat (unmarked American Pottery), $65.00; Timothy Mouse 38, $125.00; Dumbo 41* (unmarked American Pottery, 41 is the Vernon identifying number), $65.00.

Pictured are all known *Fantasia* vases and bowls designed by Walt Disney and made by Vernon Kilns. Various solid colors have been reported for most of these as well as hand-decorated versions. A backstamp which includes the vase number (39) and usually an embossed number appear underglaze. For decorated vases, add $25.00 to price.

Top, left to right: 127 Winged Pegasus vase, 7½" x 12" (widest point), $165.00; 126 Goddess vase, 10½", $150.00; 121 Goldfish bowl, 6", $125.00; 124 Satyr bowl, 3½", 7" diameter, $125.00.Bottom, left to right: 120 Mushroom bowl, 2" x 7" x 12", $150.00; 122 Winged Nymph bowl, 2½" x 12" base diameter, $125.00; 123 Winged Nymph vase, 7", $150.00; 125 Sprite bowl, 3" x 10½" base diameter, $150.00.

*The Vernon Kilns mold number corresponding to this American Pottery figure is believed to be 25.

Close-up view of hand decorated 121 Goldfish bowl, $150.00.

Royal Hickman

Royal Hickman, a familiar name in the field of design, was also associated with Vernon Kilns. In January 1942 at the Pittsburgh, Pennsylvania show held in the William Penn Hotel, Vernon Kilns introduced Melinda, an elaborate dinnerware shape designed by Hickman. At the time, he was world famous for his creations in Swedish glass and artware, and noted for his animal designs for Heisey of Newark, Ohio. According to Clarence Vogel, Editor of the *Heisey Glass Newscaster* (Vol. 4, No. 6, Plymouth, Ohio), Hickman was an artist who did contract work for many companies in the fields of metal, paper, glass and pottery. He was known to have moved about the country and lived his final days in Mexico where he reportedly passed away in 1971. Vogel states too that he was an artist of exceptional ability with a very characteristic style.

Janice Pettee

Janice Pettee sculpted the rare and almost legendary movie star figurines, believed to be the only such pottery figurines ever made. The five known figures are copyrighted 1940 with the exception of Evelyn Venable. Evelyn Venable, an American leading lady of the 1930's was frequently cast in demure roles. In the writer's conversation with her, she revealed that the 11″ figure portrayed her in the costume she wore as Shirley Temple's mother in *The Little Colonel*. Miss Venable believes the figure may have been merchandized in shops where mementos of this nature were sold. Two examples of this figurine are known; one having been given to Evelyn Venable at the time it was made and the other (pictured) belonging to a private collector. Inside the glazed hollow body, stamped under glaze, reads "Approved by Evelyn Venable (signature facsimile), Sculptured by Janice Pettee (signature facsimile), VERNON KILNS, Made in U.S.A."

11″ Evelyn Venable, $200.00; 16½″ statue of Gary Cooper marked "Dusty Rivers", "'North West Mounted Police,' A Paramount Picture", $350.00; 10″ Dorothy Lamour, believed to be from the movie "Road to Rio", $250.00; 11½″ "Sergeant Bret" as played by Preston Foster in "North West Mounted Police", $200.00; "Chief Big Bear", the part played by Walter Hampden in "North West Mounted Police", $250.00. Incidentally, Royal Doulton makes an Indian figurine today of similar quality, size, position and detail. The Vernon Kilns figurines are all marked "Sculptured by Janice Pettee" (signature facsimile) and "Vernon Potteries, Ltd." (except for figure of Evelyn Venable marked "Vernon Kilns"). All are marked "approved by" and the respective movie star's printed signature. Edward Fischer, Vernon Kilns last President also recalled a figure of Bette Davis, and a late report confirms one of Madelyn Carroll. There may be others.

Other Artists

Of all the artists, **Paul L. Davidson** must have had the longest tenure. The earliest known dated commemorative plate *The Arkansas Traveler* (copyrighted 1936), is signed by Paul Davidson. His work also included the Winchester '73 designs for dinnerware in 1950 made to coordinate with Heisey's etched glass designs of the same name.

Allen F. Brewer, Jr. of Lexington, Kentucky, internationally known for his equestrian art, designed two **Race Horse** series for hostess tableware sets: Coaltown and Greyhound, picturing famous horses, his signature on the face of every plate. According to a 1950 company catalog this series included two sizes of plates, 10½″ at $3.00 and 8½″ at $2.00 and cups and saucers at $3.00 per set. It is relatively scarce.

Orpha Klinker, Iowa born and raised in California, was best known for her painted historical and desert subjects and portraits. She had studied in America and Europe and was an academacian from American International Academy, Washington, D.C., was listed in *Who's Who in American Art, 1962*, and received honors in France, Belgium, Mexico and India. Her paintings were in the collections of Winston Churchill, Franklin Delano Roosevelt and Edgar Bergen to whom she also gave art lessons. Was it coincidence that one of Bergen's famous dummies was "Effie Klinker"? Klinker's artwork and signature appear on many of Vernon Kilns specialty ware.

Early in the 1940's a young **Mr. Cavett** (no one remembered his first name) had his art career cut short when he took a leave of absence from his job at Vernon Kilns to join the military. He was killed while in training for the paratroopers. He is best known for the very popular **Bit** series, most of which carry his name in the lower right-hand corner of the plate.

In the 1950's **Sharon Merrill** and **Jean Ames** designed striking dinnerware designs. In 1952, **Elliott House** was Art Director and is believed to have remained with the company until it went out of business.

Other artists were L. Hicks who designed the **Cocktail Hour** series, Nick Goode, Annette Honeywell, Frank Bauer*, Eugene Derdeyn, H. Fennell, Erik Sederling, Margaret Pearson Joyner, D. Klein, Joe C. Sewell, Mary Van Gelder, R. Schepe, T.R.N. Kingston, and Mary Petty, and more that are not named here.

There were many unnamed employees with an artistic flair who worked on the production line handpainting the popular patterns such as Brown Eyed Susan and the Plaids.

Though none are signed, there was a series of vases and bowls produced, some hand decorated (19) and some solid color (12) during this same period. They are similar to the Walt Disney items and are numbered upward from the Disney numbers.

Disney bowls are numbered 120 through 127. These pottery items begin with number 130, skipping to 142. There are probably bowls or vases to match the missing numbers.

Vases and bowls, not artist signed. For decorated vases, add $5.00-10.00.

Top, left to right:
135 flower bowl, 10½ ", $18.00; 134 decorated figural bird bowl, 8 ", $35.00.

Center, left to right:
130 bowl, 6½ ", $12.00.

Bottom, left to right:
142 decorated duck bowl, 13 ", $50.00; 141 ash tray, 8½ ", $15.00; 138 decorated wave bowl, 11½ ", $30.00.

*Frank Bauer was reported to have done much of the sets for *Gone With the Wind* movie.

Also known is a 139 10″ petal-shaped bowl in solid color. This bowl has also been reported as a serving dish in the Melinda dinnerware group, specifically in deep blue Blossom Time pattern.

THE WAR YEARS, POSTWAR FIRES AND RECONSTRUCTION

By 1940 Vernon Kilns was well established in two lines of production: specialty plates and dinnerware. However, during the early war years, the future of the pottery business looked bleak with so many employees going into the armed forces or the vital defense industry. High school boys were hired to supplement the work force and were willing workers. English, German and Japanese pottery imports were not available during those years and there was increased demand for dinnerware. Vernon Kilns was quick to take advantage of this situation and designed new molds and patterns nearly duplicating English patterns to meet the demand of American housewives wanting to match their English dishes. Specialty wares with patriotic themes were also in big demand. Thus, the company was able to keep production at a peak.

After the war, a fire occurred in 1946 burning half of the main building which was soon rebuilt. In 1947, two days after Christmas, a second devastating fire hit the 30-year old wood and sheet metal structures, burning everything to the ground. This fire was caused by a rupture of the main gas line going through the center of the building. The plant had been closed down for the Christmas holidays, which was traditional, in order to repair equipment and take inventory. The factory building was fully insured for over a million dollars. Mr. Bennison considered retiring at the time and dissolving the company, but, according to him, Eddie Fischer and key employees urged him to rebuild the plant. The employees were willing to take a cut in pay to keep things going rather than work elsewhere. The decision was made to rebuild the factory and carry on with the business.

With the rebuilding of a 130,000 square foot factory, all the old beehive kilns were replaced by tunnel kilns with tracks and cars rolling on the tracks. A car loaded with ware took 54 hours to go through the kilns at about 1800° plus. The system greatly increased the overall capacity of the factory.

The new building was a modern plant of steel-reinforced concrete and had an automatic sprinkler system. Suppliers of the equipment sent representatives from all over the country to Vernon, California, to view the model plant and the equipment as the very latest innovations devised by Vernon Kilns. For a short period, memento plates and ash trays were given free to visitors to the new factory.

MANUFACTURING PROCESS

As was the case in the old plant, only top grade materials were used at Vernon Kilns. An adhesive-type ball clay from Tennessee was one of the favorite clays as well as English, Kentucky and North Carolina varieties. The clays were stored in clay bins adjacent to the railroad spur in back of the plant. From the storage bins, the clay was conveyed to the vats immediately inside. Water was added for the mixing process and formed into slip which was pumped into a filter press, the function of which was to squeeze out the water. From there the clay went into a pug machine to be de-aired.

It then formed a consistency that could be worked into 10″ or 12″ rolls. The rolls were transferred to the jigger. The jiggerman would take a handful of batter and with a bat flatten it on the plaster of paris mold, in the same method as the old Poxon factory. This would form the plate and while on the revolving mold, the edges were trimmed. After the bisque was decorated it was fired in the bisque kiln at high temperatures. Finally the glaze was applied and a second high firing in the gloss kiln completed the process.

The glazes were made from silica mined in central California and were, like the clays, of very good quality. The glazes were guaranteed against crazing for twenty-five years. They have stood the test of time.

The decorating was done by hand on patterns such as Brown Eyed Susan, the Plaids, and Barkwood. No two pieces will be found identical. The method for other patterns such as the earlier Blanding, Kent and Disney dinnerware and the specialty ware was much the same as that invented in the 1750's in Liverpool, England to produce historical Staffordshire transfer-printed pottery. The designs were printed on special paper which was etched on to a copper cylinder. The roll revolved, printing an outline on tissue-like paper transfers sheets, picking up ink as it revolved and transferring the drawing to the bisque pottery, much like a printing press. The plain print was hand-tinted on some patterns and specialty ware which was termed "print and fill-in" in the industry. The plain print (plain indicating not hand-tinted) was mostly produced in colors of blue, brown or maroon on a cream background. Some was produced in green, purple or orange print on a cream background. Vernon Kilns used the same hand-painted backstamps for the print and fill-in designs as for the painted patterns.

Vernon Kilns was a pioneer in the transfer-print process. Frederick Rhead in his *Report of the Art and Design Committee* at the *U.S. Potters Association 61st Annual Convention*, in January 1940, remarked that Vernon Kilns underglaze printing was "another advance in the history of American Ceramic development . . . we may find increased interest in underglaze printing either from etched or engraved rolls." In the Our America dinnerware pattern which had over thirty designs, it became very costly.

SPECIALTY WARE

Today many people identify Vernon Kilns with its transfer-print specialty ware. Beginning in the 1930's, vast amounts were made, either stock items or special order.

Stock Items

10½″ plates - these were readily accessible to shop owners, generally in minimum orders of 100, mixed or matched, and executed on several shapes (Montecito, Melinda, San Fernando or Ultra - see Dinnerware Section for these shapes). The Ultra shape was sometimes modified. The dipped rim was flattened or turned up. Backstamps were varied: a descriptive paragraph, a State seal and/or simply "by Vernon Kilns, U.S.A.", (and occasionally without the Vernon Kilns mark, if requested by a jobber, more on that later.)

Until 1953, stock plates were plain print (PP). Colors were chiefly maroon, blue or brown on a cream background. In 1953 "handpainted" (HP) plates were added as stock items. According to company price lists, "handpainted" meant hand tinted (print and fill-in). In 1954 only handpainted plates were stock. Plain print was available only by special order (SO) and by 1955 only in minimum lots of 1000 of each subject (SO-M). For the years 1950 through 1956 (information was not available for 1951 and 1952) the following chart with code indicates availability and prices, the information was obtained from company price lists:

	1950	1953	1954	1955	1956
State Picture. All states including District of Columbia; 2 for Alaska (the Bear and the Husky). In 1950 Alabama was not available.	PP 1.75	PP 1.85 HP 2.50	HP 2.75* PP SO	HP 2.75* PP SO-M	HP 2.95* PP SO-M
State Map. All states except Hawaii (Alabama uncertain). Also a state map of the entire U.S.	PP 1.75	PP 1.85 HP 2.50	PP SO	---	---
Cities. Los Angeles, San Francisco, Phoenix, Hollywood, and Washington, D.C. Many more city plates are known, some of which may have been stock items before 1950.	PP 1.75	PP 1.85 HP 2.50	---	---	---
Famous Men. F.D. Roosevelt, Teddy Roosevelt, Woodrow Wilson, George Washington, Abraham Lincoln**, Andrew Jackson, The Atlantic Charter with Roosevelt and Churchill, Robert E. Lee, Stonewall Jackson, Will Rogers, and the President Gallery*** (all presidents on one plate, at least two 10½" editions known.)	PP 1.75	PP 1.85 HP 2.50	---	---	---
Special. The Missions*** (all California missions pictured on one plate), Cable Car San Francisco, Our West, Yellowstone Park**, Mount Rushmore**, Mother Lode and Deep in the Heart of Texas.	PP 1.75	PP 1.85 HP 2.50			
California Centennial. Transportation, El Camino Real, State Capitol, Discovery of Gold, Campo de Cahuengo and Historical Trees.	PP 1.75				
California Commemoratives. 10 in Series: Marshall Discovers Gold at Coloma 1848; University of California, Berkeley, 1873; Bear Flag Raised at Sonoma; Santa	PP 1.75				

Barbara Mission 1786; Golden Gate 1855; Pico Capitulates to Fremont 1848; Monterey (first capitol of California) 1850; Cabrillo Discovers California 1542; Cradle Rocking During Gold Rush 1849; and San Francisco Bay 1849.

Commemoratives. Only one listed in company 1953 Price List: St. Mary's in the Mountains in Virginia City, Nevada.	PP 1.85 HP 2.50
Universities. University of Notre Dame, University of Ohio, University of Michigan, only ones listed in 1953 company price list. (see list of all known colleges and schools on page 41)	PP 1.85 HP 2.50

*Alaska was the only state not included in hand painted stock.
**8½" plates of same subject were available in another version through special order.
***12½" plate of same subject available through special order or perhaps was stock item.

8½" plates -- Probably one of the most popular stock items with collectors is the **Bit** series. The series represented six different regions of the United States and was named for the respective region. Each region's series consisted of eight 8½" plates with hand-tinted scenes and burgundy bands on the rim, plus a 14" chop plate which repeated one of the scenes (an exception is the **Old Northwest** series, a chop plate is not listed in the company price lists.) Most plates bear the Cavett signature and are executed on the Ultra shape with rims often flattened or turned up. These probably were first introduced around 1940 since Cavett was an artist for Vernon Kilns at that time. The series was not listed in company price lists after 1950. In 1950 plates were priced at $1.75 each for the 8½" size and $6.50 for the 14" size.

Bits of Old New England
The Old Covered Bridge
Haying
Sunday Morning
The Cove
Old Dobbin
The Whaler
*Tapping for Sugar
Lighthouse

Bits of the Middle West
End of the Drought
Saturday Night
The Mail Train
The County Fair Blue Ribbon
The Corn Huskers
River Commerce
*R.F.D.
Fourth of July

Bits of the Old South
*Down on the Levee
Off to the Hunt
A Southern Mansion
Cypress Swamp
The Old Mill
Tobacco Field
Houseboat on the River
Cotton Patch

Bits of the Old West
The Fleecing
*The Horse Thieves
The Train Robbers
The Stage Arrival
The Stage Robbers
The Bar Fly
Thirst
The Posse

Bits of the Old Southwest
*Pueblo
Grinding Meal
Blanket Weavers
Hogan Dwellers
Baking Bread
Medicine Man
Basket Weaver
The Potters

Bits of the Old Northwest
Branding Time
Come and Get It
Fur Trapper
Logging
Logging Train
Logging Jam
Sheep Herder
Unloading the Nets
(No chop plate)

*Pattern on the chop plate.

Another in the **Bit** series was **Bits of Old England**, showing scenes from Old England. Except for the 14″ chop plate, *Golden Spur*, these were not titled but numbered one to eight.

Bits of Old England
#1 through #8
14″ *Golden Spur* chop plate

California Missions was still another in the **Bit** series. Sixteen missions were pictured plus a 14″ chop plate, a repeat of one of the 8½″ scenes. (A 12″ chop plate with the same scene has been reported executed on Melinda shape which probably was special order.) This series, like the others, appeared on the Ultra shape and in the same hand-tinted colors.

California Missions
San Fernando Rey
San Juan Capistrano
San Gabriel Archangel
Santa Barbara
*San Diego de Alcala
La Purisima Concepcion
San Buenaventura
San Luis Obispo de Tolosa
San Francisco Solano
Carmel, San Carlos Borromeo
Santa Clara
San Rafael Archangel
Santa Cruz
San Jose de Guadalupe
Dolores
San Juan Bautista

Several other individual plates were done in the **Bit** style, such as the *Virginia & Truckee Railroad* and *Avalon Bay, Santa Catalina Island*.

*Chop plate has this scene.

French Opera Reproductions. This is a series of eight plates which were reproductions of 19th century French plates depicting scenes from eight operas. In the original French series, there were twelve scenes. In the Vernon Kilns series of eight, numbered 1, 3, 5, 6, 7, 9, 10, and 12, operas numbered 2, 4, 8, and 11 were not reproduced. A 14″ chop plate with the #3 scene was also made for this series.

The artist signature on the face of the plates is also reproduced from the original, and is not a Vernon Kilns artist. Another company in the United States having the trademark "PV" (Pleasant Village) also reproduced the plates for an importer, Mitteldorfer Straus, Inc. of New York City, which has caused some confusion to collectors. Though sometimes difficult to distinguish the "PV" plates from Vernon Kilns on the surface, Vernon's are backstamped "French Reproductions by Vernon Kilns, U.S.A." This series is executed on the Ultra shape (sometimes the rim is flattened) and is hand-tinted. The Vernon Kilns operas are: *No. 1 Le Pre Aux Clercs; No. 3 Le Barbier de Seville; No. 5 Guillaume Tell; No. 6 Les Dragons de Villars; No. 7 La Dame Blanche; No. 9 Lucie de Lammermoor; No. 10 La Musette de Portici; No. 12 Faust.*

Music Masters featured portraits of the great composers with a facsimile of the composer's signature on each plate. An actual score of music composed by each forms the border. A short biography is on the reverse side. Found in sepia brown tones on a cream background and executed on the Ultra shape, they listed at $1.25 each in 1950. A series of eight, they are: *Peter Tschaikovsky; Ludwig van Beethoven; Felix Mendelssohn; Edvard Grieg; Ignace Jan Paderewski; Frans Schubert; Fredric Chopin; Franz Liszt.*

The **Cocktail Hour** is a series of eight different subjects in sepia brown on a cream background on the Ultra shape. They listed for $1.25 each in 1950. Each pictured a young lady with the border design featuring the names of various drinks (L. Hicks, artist). They are as follows: *Bacardi; The Bronx; Hot Toddy; Manhattan; Old Fashioned; Pink Lady; Singapore Sling; Whiskey Sour.*

Mother Goose is a single plate described in the company price list as in "deep pink only." However, the one pictured is brown and depicts nursery rhyme figures. It originally sold for $1.25. It is now scarce.

Race Horse Series. Coaltown and Greyhound hostess sets were available in 1950. Each artwork was signed on the face by internationally famed equestrian artist, Allen F. Brewer, Jr. The sets consisted of hand-tinted 10½″ and 8½″ plates and cup and saucer ($3.00 each in 1950.) These are considered scarce. A 10½″ plate has been reported which pictures a trotter with driver and sulky and under the picture are the words "Trotter, Greyhound 1:55¼, Sep Palin up" ("up" meaning driver). The paragraph on the back of the plate reads, "The world's champion trotter, grey gelding foaled 1932 by Guy Abbey-Elizabeth. Bred by Mr. Henry H. Knight's Almahurst Farm, Nicholasville, KY. Owned by E.J. Baker, St. Charles, Illinois. Developed and raced by Sep Palin. During the racing career of Greyhound, Harness racing saw its greatest champion establish 16 world records. The grey gelding proved unbeatable through his long campaign, establishing himself as undisputed King of the Grand Circuit. . . .At Lexington, Kentucky in 1938, reinsman Sep Palin drove Greyhound in his historic tilt against time, and the son of Guy Abbey trotted the fastest mile ever recorded in trotting annal . . . 1:55¼."

Christmas Series. This series is believed to have been stock, but the date they were available is not known. There were three motifs: Santa Claus, Vernon's Christmas Tree, Ye Old Tyme (also sometimes captioned "Christmas" and in one case known to have been special ordered for "The Austin Family"). Artist L. Hicks's signature appears on the face of one of this series. Original price is not known. 10½" plates and cups and saucers have been found.

Spoon holders were available for a while in the 1950's, subjects and price not known.

Miniature plates, 4¼", having the same subjects as the 10½" plates are included under Stock items. However, it is not known if they actually were stock or when they were available.

Ash trays, 5½", were available in deep pink, blue or brown on an ivory background and have the same subjects as the 10½" plates. (According to the 1950 price list, the ash trays sold for 85 cents.) Other subjects reported are: a memento of visit to the factory, universities, cities, airplanes, commemoratives and even foreign countries. These were special ordered.

After dinner (demitasse) cups and saucers. These were an assortment of 24 views of **Scenic America** subjects, in colors of brown, pink and purple print with hand-tinted scenic panel borders. These came packaged in a special carton and sold for 85 cents each. A six-color counter card displayed three different shapes: Melinda, Montecito and San Fernando. They are: *Washington Monument, Washington, D.C.; Grand Canyon, Arizona; Christ Church, Virginia; Jefferson Davis's Home, Virginia; Apache Trail, Arizona; Little White House, Georgia; Singing Tower, Lake Wales, Florida; Monterey Cypress, Carmel, California; Monticello, T. Jefferson Home, Virginia; My Old Kentucky Home; Jefferson Memorial, Washington, D.C.; Andrew Jackson Home, Tennessee; Statue of Liberty, New York; Natural Bridge, Virginia; Cypress Gardens, Florida; Mt. Vernon, Washington's Home; Niagara Falls, New York; Monument Valley, Arizona; Plantation Home, South Carolina; Lone Cypress, Carmel, California; University of Virginia; Mississippi River Steamboat; First Confederate White House, Alabama; Lookout Mountain, Tennessee.*

There were probably some that were special order designs as others have been reported such as *Ft. McHenry, Old Faithful,* and *Forest Lawn.*

Special Order

Literally hundreds of designs and items were created on special request, many marked "Made expressly" or "especially for" and "by Vernon Kilns", sometimes the Vernon Kilns name was omitted. Some plates have been reported backstamped "Capsco Product" (Capitol Souvenir Company, Washington, D.C.) and usually without the Vernon Kilns name, or "Wesco Kilns" (West Coast Kilns). Capsco also ordered souvenir plates from Adams of England.

Cities. 10½" plates of cities were popular subjects for special order as there were fewer city plates available as stock items. In 1974 a collector in California had gathered 51 city plates. A few that have been reported are: *The Tri-Cities* -- Davenport, Iowa, Rock Island, Illinois, and Moline, Illinois, made for Peterson-Harned-Von Maur, Davenport, Iowa; *San Antonio, Texas, Home of the Alamo,* designed for The Vogue; and two for Philadelphia. Altogether, Texas probably ordered more plates than any other state.

Famous Men. This category was also popular for special designs. Some 10½" plates were: *Generalissimo and Madame Chiang Kai-shek* (backstamped "A CDGC Creation, Made in U.S.A.); *General Douglas MacArthur; Jefferson Davis,* President of Confederate States; and *William Pryor Letchworth.*

Universities and Schools. Quite a number of college and school 10½″ plates have been reported, namely: *John Brown University*, Arkansas; *Christian College* in Columbia, Missouri; *Brigham Young University*, Utah; *Culver School for Boys; Duke University* (also ash tray); *Fresno State College*, California (8½″ plate); *Girard College of Philadelphia; University of Idaho; University of Illinois; Iowa State College; Iowa State University; University of Illinois; Iowa State College; Iowa State University; University of Kansas; Lincoln Memorial University*, Tennessee; *Michigan State College; University of Michigan; University of Missouri; University of North Carolina; University of Notre Dame; University of Ohio; Oklahoma Baptist University; Oregon State College Diamond Jubilee; Pacific University of Forest Grove*, Oregon; *Purdue University; University of Southern California; Southern Methodist University; Stanford University; Texas State College for Women*, 1st Edition, 1953; *University of Texas; University of Virginia; University of Washington; Whitman College in Walla Walla, Washington; Stephen F. Austin State College*, Texas; and *University of Wisconsin*. Some such as the *Stanford* plate may not bear the Vernon Kilns backstamp. A college fraternity, Sigma Alpha Epsilon, ordered plates in purple print and the Rotary Club of Vernon ordered large plates, ewers and coffee servers decorated with members signatures and Rotary insignia.

World War II Commemoratives were popular subjects during these years. One frequently seen is of wartime hero, General Douglas MacArthur. *"Remember Pearl Harbor"* is another but does not have the Vernon Kilns mark. It is backstamped "Made in U.S.A., Exclusive Distributors China and Glass Co., New Orleans, La." The artist was Margaret Pearson Joyner.

Religious organizations placed special orders. Some plates known are: *History of Catholic Church*, 1950; *Old Cathedral in Vincennes, Indiana; Catholic Churches of the Rio Grande Valley, Texas; Episcopal Churches of Rio Grande Valley;* and *the Relief Society Centennial Commemorative of the Church of Jesus Christ of Latter Day Saints*. Forest Lawn Cemetery in Glendale, California ordered several different items including demitasse cups and saucers featuring their Church of Redemption and an 8½″ plate of the Wee Church of the Heather. The Forest Lawn items did not carry the Vernon Kilns backstamp.

Convention plates were special ordered, such as the large plate for the *Republican Convention of 1956* held in the State of California and given by the host state to the attending delegates. Others were 10½″ plates: *Al Malaikah Imperial Council Session, Los Angeles, 1950*, which pictures the late movie star, Harold Lloyd, Imperial Potentate at that time; *Indiana Grand Chapter Order Eastern Star, 75th Anniversary, 1949; Lions International Chicago 1950; 46th Convention of Postmasters, St. Louis 1950; 48th Convention of Postmasters 1952, Boston* (Paul Davidson, artist). 8½″ plates were: *Texas Federation of Music Clubs, 5th District 1949* and *American Society of Civil Engineers at Houston, 1951*.

Transportation. Airplane and train 10½″ plates are very popular with collectors (ashtrays also were made with some of the same subjects). An 8½″ plate featuring the "Virginia & Truckee RR -- Route to Comstock" was done in the "Bit" style. Other transportation-type plates were the *Chicago Railroad Fair, 1950** (two different designed plates were created for the Fair on special order); *Detroit, Home of General Motors; Merry Oldsmobile;* and the *San Francisco Cable Car*.

Advertising Items. Examples on page 62 are two Trader Vic Restaurant pieces and a 1950 Coca Cola bowl (alongside a figural Penguin bottle which was not an advertising item but an early Vernon Kilns novelty item.) 10½" plates were made for La Belle Baker's Chocolate in two editions, 1940 and 1941, and are sought after by both Baker's Chocolate and Vernon Kilns collectors. The Shamrock Hotel in Texas ordered an attractive plate designed for them in green print with a shamrock border.

Souvenirs. Dinnerware sets or individual pieces (cups and saucers, pitchers, etc.) were ordered to be sold as souvenirs at popular tourist areas like Yosemite, Alaska, Mt. Rushmore, and Lake Tahoe. A ½ pint pitcher (Melinda shape) depicting in full color the totem pole against a backdrop of green fir trees at Ketchikan, Alaska, was made exclusively for Hall's Trading Post by Vernon Kilns. Many commemorative plates of historical places were designed: *Williamsburg, Virginia; Colonial Annapolis, Maryland; Historic Boston;* and *Excelsior Springs, Missouri* among others. Two turnpikes were commemorated, the New Jersey and the Pennsylvania.

Foreign countries also ordered picture plates and ash trays. Two 10½" plates are known: *Caracas, Venezuela* which pictures Estatua del Libertodor surrounded by city buildings and backstamped in Spanish "Disenado por Vernon Kilns, Los Angeles, Calif.", and the other was *El Paso, Jaurez.* An ash tray backstamped "Flota Mercante Grancolombiana, S.A., Venezuela, Colombia, Ecuador" pictures the National Monument, buildings and a Santiago steamer. A dinnerware set of four place settings (cups, saucers, dessert and dinner plates) has been reported. Described as a scenic; a map in the center, the words "West Indies" on the left, "East Indies" in the right, and two red ships under full sail on blue water. Green and yellow spices, nutmeg, mace and pepper are at top and bottom and the names of spices are around the border. Though not backstamped Vernon Kilns, it is reported to be unquestionably their product. The mark is a circle similar to mark 19, with the words "da Bron, Handpainted, Spice Islands (pattern name apparently), Underglaze, Made in California, U.S.A."

Oddities have been reported such as an Historic Natchez, Mississippi plate having two artist signatures, Eugene Derdeyn at lower left and Paul L. Davidson, upper right; and an Ohio plate signed by both Schepe and Cavett. Two different plates were done of the San Jacinto Memorial Monument, one by Schepe and one by Goode. One Statue of Liberty was done by Orpha Klinker and another by Paul Davidson.

Historic Baltimore, a series of eight 8½" plates in blue or maroon print that was made exclusively for Hutzler Brothers Company has been reported. The plates in this series are: *#1 Carroll Mansion "Homewood", #2 Baltimore Harbor, #3 University of Maryland School of Medicine, #4 Johns Hopkins Hospital, #5 Fort McHenry, #6 Court House and Battle Monument, #7 Washington Monument,* and *#8 Old Shot Tower.*

This section of the book has only touched upon a few representative examples and descriptions of the many hundreds of commemoratives made by Vernon Kilns over a period of twenty years. It is the goal of a newly formed group of collectors to document all commemoratives ever made (if this is indeed possible) through their *Vernon Views Newsletter*, P.O. Box 945, Scottsdale, Arizona 85252.

These next 2 photographs picture 10½ ″ plates executed on the Ultra shape and backstamped "by Vernon Kilns, U.S.A.", exceptions noted. Special order items were usually backstamped "Made Exclusively for . . ." or words to that effect.

States and Cities

Top, left to right:
Mississippi 5½ ″ ash tray, $10.00; *Alaska Husky* 4¼ ″ mini plate (Orpha Klinker, artist), $15.00; *Oklahoma* map portraying famous places, $15.00; *Detroit, Michigan*, 5½ ″ ash tray (Orpha Klinker, artist), "Made Exclusively for The J.L. Hudson Co.", $10.00.

2nd row, left to right:
Flint, Michigan, Home of General Motors, "Made Expressly for McLogan & Austin, The China Closet", border design of 1950 vintage automobiles, $15.00; *Honolulu*, pre-statehood, hand-tinted, (Orpha Klinker, artist), $18.00; *Memphis, Tennessee*, "Designed for The John Gerber Company", pictures Colonel Memphis, $15.00.

3rd row, left to right:
Vermont, Green Mountain State (H. Goode, artist), pictures 30th President Calvin Coolidge, and Freeman's Oath paragraph backstamp, $15.00; *Omaha's 100th Birthday, 1854-1954* (Paul Davidson, artist), hand-tinted pictures of famous places and farm products, Story of Omaha on backstamp, $18.00; *Kentucky Blue Grass State*, pictures race horse and places of interest, $15.00.

Bottom, left to right:
Chicago picturing the Marshall Field Clock plus points of interest, "Made Exclusively for Marshall Field & Co.", $15.00; *Seattle Washington*, (Orpha Klinker, artist), illustrates Seattle's scenic beauty, backstamp states "Seattle, found in 1851 . . .", plate dated 1941, $15.00; *Alaska Bear Commonwealth* (prior to statehood), backstamp reads " . . . 1867 . . . purchased from Russia for $7,200,000.", $15.00. *Note:* Vernon Kilns produced the identical Alaska Bear plate with two other different backstamps, one "U.S.A." only, and the other "Designed for Westco Kilns, U.S.A.", neither marked Vernon Kilns.

Presidents, Civic Clubs, and World War II

Top, left to right:
Abraham Lincoln, the 16th President, backstamp gives his birth and death dates and a paragraph from his Second Inaugural Address, "With malice toward none, with charity for all . . ." (Melinda shape), $18.00; *Lincoln Memorial*, 8½" plate pictures the Lincoln Monument in Washington, D.C. (artist Joe C. Sewell) backstamped "Fourscore and seven years ago . . ." and "The Earthly Pilgrimage of Abraham Lincoln". $25.00.

2nd row, left to right:
The United States in Action, (Goode, artist), hand-tinted print picturing branches of armed forces in combat surrounding F.D. Roosevelt's portrait, Commander of Armed Forces, backstamp reads "With confidence in our armed forces -- with the unbounding determination of our people -- we will gain the inevitable triumph -- so help us God . . ." (from Roosevelt's first war address December 8, 1941, 12:30 p.m. at a joint session of Congress after the attack on Pearl Harbor), First Edition 1942, $25.00; *Presidential* plate, emphasis on war time (Cavett, artist), backstamp is paragraph from "Declaration of War Against the Axis", $18.00; *George Washington, the Father of His Country, 1789-1797* (Cavett, artist), depicts scenes from his life, backstamp gives birth and death dates and paragraph from his Farewell Address, $18.00.

3rd row, left to right:
Coffee Server decorated with Rotary Club International's insignia and signatures of members of Vernon City Rotary Club, circa 1953, backstamp reads "Made for City of Vernon Rotary Club", $45.00, (other items found that were made for the Vernon Rotary Club are a large platter, pitcher, and 5½" bowl); *Presidential Gallery No.2*, pictures all presidents including Dwight D. Eisenhower, 1953, and Presidential Seal (Paul Davidson, artist), $18.00; *Our Presidential Gallery* picturing all presidents with George Washington in center and includes Harry S. Truman, 1945, $18.00.

Bottom, left to right:
Airborne Division, portrays a parachute trooper on the ground in combat position and five Airborne Division patches, backstamp paragraph reads "For the men of five Airborne Divisions and the troopers of the unattached Parachute Regiments and Battalions who jumped and glided into combat, charged with savage fury . . . this plate was designed by David K. Webster and manufactured by Vernon Kilns, Los Angeles, California. Yours was the Glory: To battle fear and conquer Fascism", (Montecito shape), $25.00; *Our Presidential Gallery*, First Edition, 1942, 12½" plate, "made expressly for Everlast Metal Products Co.", (almost identical design to Presidential Gallery above except Mt. Vernon is pictured in place of Truman), $25.00; *Remember Pearl Harbor, On to Victory* (artist Margaret Pearson Joyner), not marked Vernon Kilns, $25.00.

"Bit" series 8½ " plates and "Race Horse" examples. "Bit" plates are usually marked "Bits of the (region)", title, and "designed, copyrighted and engraved by Vernon Kilns, U.S.A." These 8½ ""Bit" plates are $20.00-35.00 each.

Top, left to right:
Off to the Hunt, Old South; *#4*, Old England; *San Juan Capistrano*, California Missions.

2nd row, left to right:
The Cove, Tapping for Sugar, and *The Old Lighthouse* -- all Old New England series.

3rd row, left to right:
Stage Robbers, Thirst -- both Old West; *Baking Bread*, Old Southwest.

Bottom, left to right:
Greyhound 1:55¼, 6½ " saucer, $6.50; *Horse Thieves*, Old West, 14 " chop plate, $45.00-55.00; Coaltown, 6½ " saucer, $6.50. Race Horse items are marked "Made by Vernon Kilns, U.S.A."

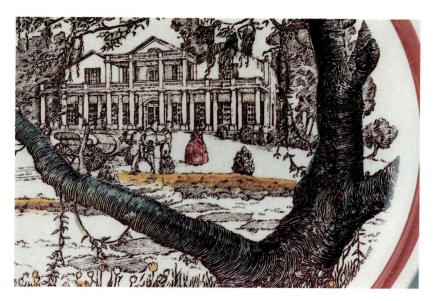

Close-up view of *A Southern Mansion*, **Old South**, showing Cavett signature, $25.00.

Bit plates.

Top, left to right: *Virginia & Truckee RR, Route to the Comstock*, pictures old No. 11 'The Reno" engine, backstamp paragraph reads ". . . The Reno was used for passenger service between Reno, Carson City, and Virginia City from 1872, service discontinued in the late 1930's. The No. 11 built in 1872 at a cost of $12,250, on March 1945 sold to MGM Studios where it has been used in the filming of motion picture "Union Pacific", $35.00; *Avalon Bay* view, Santa Catalina Island, $25.00. Bottom, left to right: *San Juan Bautista; San Jose de Guadalupe, San Carlos Borromeo, Carmel* (all three are from the **Mission** series and are by Orpha Klinker), $25.00 each.

50

8½″ Stock items.

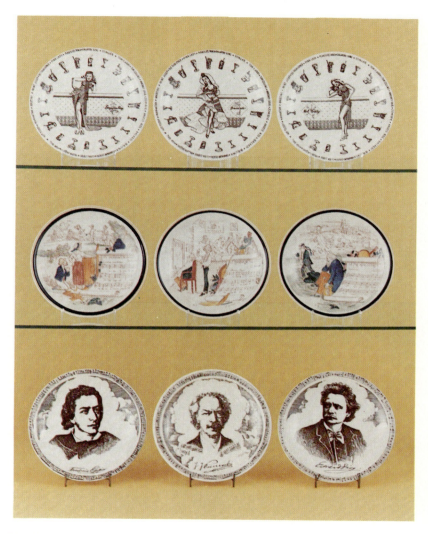

Top, left to right:
Cocktail Hour: *Singapore Sling, Bacardi, Hot Toddy.* $20.00 each.

2nd row, left to right:
French Opera Reproductions: *#6 Les Dragons de Villars, #3 Le Barbier de Seville, #1 Le Pre Aux Clercs.* $20.00 each.

3rd row, left to right:
Music Masters: *Frederick Chopin, Ignace Jan Paderewski, Edvard Grieg.* $20.00 each.

Top row, left to right:
Ye Old Tymes tea cup and saucer, $12.50 (matching 10½" plate in row 3); Old Faithful after dinner cup and saucer (San Fernando shape), a special order item of the Scenic America series, $15.00; special order 5" vase picturing baseball player and words "American Ceramic Society, Southern California Section, Annual Sports Day, July 16, 1955, Lakewood Country Club", backstamped "donated by Vernon Kilns", $25.00, scarce; Vernon's Christmas Tree cup and saucer, $15.00 (has a matching 10½" plate).

2nd row, left to right:
The Arkansas Traveler 10½" plate (Paul Davidson's initials only), copyright date 1936, backstamped "R.E. McCann, Ft. Smith, Arkansas", $18.00; pair salt and pepper shakers (unmarked Montecito shape) pictures Half Dome and reported to be from a breakfast set that was decorated with different scenes of Yosemite National Park, $12.00 pair, scarce; *Dorchester, Massachusetts, Circa 1773* commissioned by Walter Baker & Co., Inc. to mark their 175th anniversary, pictures in deep blue the Village and Mill in which James Baker and John Hannan manufactured the first chocolate in America in 1765. Outstanding historical significance and indeed a treasure for Baker's Chocolate as well as Vernon historical plate collectors. Backstamped "First Edition, 1940" and pictures the "La Belle Chocolatiere" famous trademark. Second Edition is dated 1941 and is not as deep blue. First Edition, $35.00. Second Edition, $25.00; 1949 Easter Fires of Fredericksburg, Texas. Another scarce plate*, this one features bunnies preparing eggs for distribution to children against background of church steeples and roof-tops of Fredericksburg and Cross Mountain where Easter fires flare. Backstamped " . . . century old custom based on folklore and tradition . . .", $35.00.

3rd row, left to right:
Vernon's Santa Claus 10½" plate, $25.00, and matching cup and saucer, $15.00; Vernon Kilns Bowling League, 1956 tumbler (Anytime shape), pictures ball and pins, backstamped "Donated by Vernon Kilns", $18.00, rare; Christmas plate (L. Hicks, artist's name is on the mailbox), Ye Old Tymes motif, $20.00.

Bottom, left to right: 8½" plates: French Opera Reproduction #6 *Les Dragons de Villars*, $20.00; Memento given to visitors to the factory, pictures the new, modern plant, the original building, and popular dinnerware patterns decorate the border (L. Hicks, artist), $35.00. Backstamp has signature of Faye G. Bennison, President of Vernon Kilns; Vernon's Mother Goose (Fellepe, artist), pictures nursery rhyme figures and words "My Own Mother Goose Plate", backstamped "Boys and Girls Plate designed by Vernon Kilns", circa 1950, $35.00, scarce.

*A matching cup and saucer has been reported.

Famous People and Historic Places Commemoratives. A few plates dating from 1936 through 1956 are pictured, some special order, some stock.

Top, left to right:
Williamsburg, The Historical City pictures scenes of the restored village, "Made exclusively for Casey's, Inc.", $18.00; *The Little White House* features President Franklin Delano Roosevelt, "Made exclusively for the Little White House Souvenir Shop, Warm Springs, Georgia", $18.00.

2nd row, left to right:
Our National Capitol features the Capitol building with brief paragraph of historical facts, and the colorful maroon and blue leaf border of the Melinda shape lends itself to a maroon-transfer patriotic color scheme, $18.00; *The Symbolic Statue of Liberty* represents a land of freedom for all oppressed peoples. Backstamp reads, "The New Colossus . . .'This tablet, with her sonnet to the Bartholdi Statue of Liberty engraved upon it, is placed upon these walls in loving memory of Emma Lazarus. Born in New York City, July 22nd, 1849, Died November 19th, 1887. This plate was made expressly for James Hill, Bedloe's Island, N.Y.'", (Orpha Klinker, artist). $25.00. Another Statue of Liberty plate was designed by Paul Davidson.

Bottom, left to right:
Beloved humorist, *Will Rogers*, (1879-1935) a stock item pictures his birthplace, Santa Monica ranch and memorials (Cavett, artist), $15.00; *General Douglas MacArthur*, courageous military leader of World War II, this plate was made while he was in command of the United States Far East Forces at age 62. "Made exclusively for Barker Bros." (a Los Angeles furniture store), and also marked "First Edition 5000 plates". One might speculate this was a stock item as so many are found, however, it was not listed as late as 1950 in a company price list. $15.00.

College, Religious, Political, and Fraternal 10½ " plates.

Top row, left to right:
El Camino Real 14 " plate, designed by Annette Honeywell, First Edition, Ltd. and pictures twenty-one California missions and their founding dates all on one plate, $25.00; *Franciscan Monastary,* Washington, D.C., Commissariat of the Holy Land, double marked "A Capsco Product by Vernon Kilns", pictures monastary scenes, $18.00.

2nd row, left to right:
Michigan State College (rare green print) features campus scenes and college seal (R. Schepe, artist's signature in tree branch), backstamped "Copyright 1941, Pig 'n Whistle Gifts, East Lansing" and brief paragraph about the college, $18.00; *Sigma Alpha Epsilon* fraternity (rare purple print) showing fraternity insignia and scenes (P.L.D. artist), backstamp paragraph states ". . . the first national fraternity to originate in the South, found at University of Alabama, March 9, 1856 . . . narrowly surviving the war between the States, it soon flourished again, becoming truly national in the 1890 decade . . . ", $18.00; *Relief Society Centennial Commemorative* of the Church of Jesus Christ of Latter Day Saints pictures the first Society meeting, Nauvoo, March 17, 1842. Backstamp states ". . . oldest national women's organization in the United States organized by Joseph Smith . . .", $18.00.

3rd row, left to right:
The University of Notre Dame, hand-tinted print, pictures the Rockne Memorial Fieldhouse and halls of learning, backstamp reads in part ". . . founding in 1842" along with the University seal, $22.50; *The University of Idaho* shows campus buildings and the University seal, and backstamp reads ". . . located at Moscow, established 1889, six months before Idaho was admitted to statehood." "Made exclusively for Davids, Inc., Moscow, Idaho", $18.00; *Ohio State University* (R. Schepe, artist's signature in foliage) pictures medical center, stadium and halls of learning, backstamp includes University seal, $18.00.

Bottom, left to right:
Al Malaikah, Los Angeles, Shrine plate dated 1950 pictures Harold Lloyd (movie star), Imperial Potentate, handicapped children, Shrine Auditorium and insignia, (Erik Sederling, artist), $18.00; *1956 Republican National Convention,* 13 " handpainted souvenir plate depicts State seal and message signed by Governor Goodwin J. Knight. This was presented to attending delegates by the California State Host Committee, and the backstamp paragraph reads that the meeting marks the centennial year of the first National Convention of the Party whose first Presidential candidate was a Californian, John Fremont. This was also the first Republican Party Convention to be held in the West. This plate was found in its original cardboard box, decorated with a map of California and "Welcome to California. We hope you enjoy your visit & take this opportunity to see as much of our Golden State as possible." $65.00. In original box, $75.00.

Pictured are 10½ " plates which in the 1940's were all special order in minimum lots of 1000. Today they are scarce and prized by train and plane buffs as well as Vernon Kilns collectors. All have the Vernon Kilns, U.S.A mark. All $35.00 each.

Top, left to right:
The San Juan (Erik Sederling, artist), backstamp states in part ". . .last of its kind to remind us of the spectacular little trains that once were found running throughout the West . . ."; *The Galloping Goose* (R. Schepe, artist), paragraph on back reads "Through the rugged mountains of Southwestern Colorado serving lonely and sparsely settled areas, runs the Rio Grande Southern Railroad . . .". Shows the "Goose" as it is today and Engine No. 9 as it was in the 1890's; *The "Emma Sweeney" Star of "Ticket to Tomahawk"*, filmed in Durango and Silverton, Colorado, has statement on back: "Old Engine No. 20 of the Rio Grande Southern . . . restyled and decorated for *Ticket to Tomahawk* filmed by 20th Century Fox . . . during the summer of 1949" (Erik Sederling, artist). These three plates have a railroad track border design and are backstamped "Manufactured for Jackson Hardware, Inc. of Durango, Colorado".

2nd row, left to right:
U.S. Naval Air Station, Alameda, California, pictures 1940-era Navy propeller planes and Administration Building, backstamp includes Navy Air Force insignia and reads "The United States Naval Air Station, Alameda, California" (similar plate for the Naval Air Station at Pensacola, Florida); *In the Air--It's Convair*, pictures propeller and jet, military and passenger planes. "Made exclusively for Consolidated Vultee Aircraft Corporation, San Diego, California, Ft. Worth, Texas"; *Vultee Get 'em into the Blue*, First Edition,pictures military and one private plane, "Stinson Voyager". A descriptive paragraph on back gives brief history of Vultee Aircraft founded in 1932.

3rd row, left to right:
Lockheed Aircraft pictures both military and civilian planes of the early 1940's, backstamp gives facts about Lockheed, . . . "organized in 1926", . . . "Howard Hughes used a Lockheed for his record around-the-world flight", . . . "Designed for Lockheed Aircraft Corp., Burbank, California"; *North American Aviation*, company logo and words "Bombers-Fighters-Trainers Built the North American Way", pictures air view of factory as background for planes in the air. Backstamp gives brief history of company, founded in 1928, with factories at Inglewood, Kansas City and Dallas along with "Designed for North American Aviation"; *Douglas, First Around the World* features a B-19 amid other 1940 military planes set against a Southern California shoreline with backstamp paragraph about "The First Twenty Years" and "Designed for Douglas Aircraft Co., Inc., Santa Monica, California"and "Sold Exclusively at Henshey's, Santa Monica, California".

Bottom, left to right:
Douglas, Long Beach, California, (Margaret Pearson Joyner, artist, the only airplane plate that is artist signed) pictures early 1940 Army Cargo, B-19, Flying Fortress planes and airview of Douglas, Long Beach. Backstamp boasts "America's most modern aircraft plant . . ." "Made exclusively for Stricklin's, Long Beach"; *Martin Aircraft*, pictures among other planes, the famous China Clipper and B-26 with Maryland coast airview. Backstamp reads "The longest line of military aircraft history is the Martin Bomber . . ." "Made exclusively for Hecht Brothers, Baltimore, Maryland"; *Curtiss-Wright*, features World War II military pursuit planes in combat including U.S. Army P-40 and RAF Kittyhawk. Backstamp states "Curtiss-Wright, Aviation's Oldest Names . . . the company was incorporated in New York State in December 1910, the largest producer of aircraft during World War I . . ." "Designed for Curtiss-Wright Corporation, Airplane Division, Buffalo, Columbus, St. Louis."

Special Order Commemoratives*

Top, left to right:
Chicago Railroad Fair, "Made exclusively for Marshall Field & Company" . . . 1949 commemorating the one hundredth anniversary of railroading". Pictures engines from 1829 to the streamliner, featuring 26 railroad logos on border (Stevan, artist), $35.00; *In My Merry Oldsmobile*, commemorating the "era of horse-less carriage and the yesteryears when motoring was a heroic and adventurous feat . . . rapid development, in styles and added conveniences, through the untiring efforts of the automotive industry . . ." This is particularly nostalgic today in the light of America's faltering automobile industry. Copyrighted 1950, made for Pig 'n Whistle Gifts, East Lansing (Hicks, artist). $25.00.

2nd row, left to right:
Mark Twain commemorative features famous Twain landmarks and his portrait (Sederling, artist), $20.00; *Vallejo, California, Home of Mare Island Navy Yard*, backstamped "City was founded in 1849 by General Vallejo and was State Capitol in 1851 for two years." $18.00.

Bottom, left to right:
American Society of Civil Engineers, 8½" plate presented at 1951 Convention in Houston, Texas, $15.00; *Colorful San Francisco*, (stock item), pictures cable cars, hillsides and Chinatown. Backstamp states ". . . first cable car started on its initial run August 1, 1873 with inventor Hallidie at the grip . . . the 1906 earthquake and fire reduced cable facilities to rubble but the pint-size cars were back on the job within a few short months." $35.00.

*exceptions noted.

Advertising by Vernon Kilns.

Coca Cola 10″ bowl, circa 1950, designed to hold six bottles and crushed ice (22), $75.00; Penguin figural decanter, 9½″, circa 1933 (6), $45.00. (Decanter not an advertising item.)

Trader Vic, 9½″ plate "Designed Especially for Me, Trader Vic, (signature)", $35.00; 8½″ Mai Tai glass, figure and decoration in high relief, made for "Trader Vic's, Ltd., Honolulu, Hawaii." $45.00.

Top, left to right:
Two 10½" plates -- A reproduction painting by Paul Davidson of the actual Last Supper scenes from the staged *Black Hills Passion Play of America*, "first American performance of the World Famous Luenen Passion Play in 1932", a home was established for it in the Black Hills in 1939. Backstamp reads "copyright 1953, Janice A. Blue, Spearfish, South Dakota", $25.00; *Our West*, first edition, 1942, pictures wagon trains, land clearing, gold panning and a modern city, $18.00.

Bottom, left to right:
Cup and saucer with matching plate were made exclusively for Alaska Crippled Children's Association, each piece so marked. Plate and saucer decorated with dog sleds and Eskimo portrait, cup and borders of plates picture the animals of the far North -- bear, moose, and mountain sheep. Cup and saucer $15.00, 10½" plate, $25.00.

An unusual 10½" commemorative plate by Eskimo artist Robert Mayokok of Nome, Alaska has been reported. Native Eskimo scenes decorate the plate in black etched lines simulating scrimshaw on ivory background, executed on Melinda shape. A rare gem in Vernon Kilns commemoratives.

DINNERWARE

Artist Gale Turnbull, who became director of the art department, was hired early in 1936. New shapes and designs which were modern, simple and artistic were created by Turnbull and many times his signature appears above the Vernon Kilns backstamp (marks 33 and 34). His "peasant" style art is distinctive with a French manner adapted to native American motifs. Under his direction many famous artists created designs which made Vernon Kilns a leader in the American dinnerware market. It is believed Turnbull left Vernon Kilns about 1942. His creative influence, however, endured for the lifetime of the company.

Royal Hickman then entered the scene and in 1942 the company introduced the Melinda shape which he designed. Royal Hickman was already world-famous for his creations in Swedish glass and other art ware.

In 1952, designer Elliot House headed the art department, remaining until the close of business in 1958. He is credited with designing the Anytime shape. In the 1950's, two artists, Sharon Merrill and Jean Ames, designed attractive shapes and patterns.

Dinnerware was sold throughout the United States and Canada in better stores. Ads in national magazines, *House Beautiful, Life, Good Housekeeping, Sunset* and others attested to Vernon's superior quality, durability and light weight (compared to the heavier pottery of most contemporary manufacturers).

Because of the great quantity of patterns produced by Vernon Kilns and the limitation of space in this book, the dinnerware section has been organized into groups according to shapes and illustrated with examples of patterns and items in each shape category. In chronological order, the shapes are Montecito, Coronado, Ultra*, Melinda, San Fernando, San Marino, Lotus*, Pan American variation*, Chatelaine, Anytime* and Year 'Round*. An indexed listing of all known patterns by name, number or both is provided. However, not all pieces were made for every pattern and sizes may vary from measurements given. The earliest patterns are not included in this section but are photographed in the beginning pages. Company names for shapes are given when known. Numbers appearing after pictured items indicate mark, "U" unmarked.

*Author's description of shape in lieu of any company name.

Montecito Shape

This seems to be Vernon's own first original shape. It is not believed to be a Gale Turnbull creation because the shape was used by Harry Bird who was reported to be working at Vernon Kilns before Turnbull. Solid color patterns employing this shape were two: Early California, in bright colors, and Modern California, in soft pastels. The flatware and holloware have indented concentric rings on rims. On flatware, the rim is of medium width with one ring at rim's outer edge, two at rim's inner edge, and another within the flat surface of the plate directly beneath the flat rim. With holloware, the same is true but the outer ring creates a banded effect. In later years, the rings were much less distinct. Handles as well as overall shapes were angular in the earliest Montecito holloware. This was especially true of older Early California versus Modern California which had rounded handles and shapes. Early California was apparently later produced on the round shapes. Bird and Turnbull used both versions for their decorating. The Montecito shape had the longest run of all and was still in use in 1958.

The next two photographs show earlier examples of Early California. All bear mark 13 with exceptions noted by number in parenthesis following item. 1937 colors were yellow, turquoise, green, brown, dark blue, light blue, orange and pink. Today the most desirable colors are the orange, dark blue and brown. 1946 colors were blue, green, peach, turquoise, and yellow. Ivory is also pictured, date of production unknown. Maroon has been reported, and is scarce and very collectible. From 1950 on, Early California was not listed in available company price lists.

Top center: 3 pint tankard pitcher (10). Center, left to right: 1 pint bowl; jam jar with notched lid (10); 9" muffin tray and lid; 2 quart ice-lip disk jug (this jug shape was interchangeable with Ultra). Bottom, left to right: ¼ lb. butter tray and cover (10); double spout gravy boat with attached underplate; pepper and salt shakers (9); three oval platters, sizes 8½" (relish), 12½", and 14½".

Top, left to right: 11" grill plate (grill plates have been found decorated with floral decal and mark 8); 7½" covered casserole (diameter excluding handles), the casserole is somewhat like an old fashioned 2 lb. sugar bowl; 9½" plate. Center, left to right: Lug chowder (cereal); cup (10); saucer; 2 cup 7" demitasse pot (10); 6 cup angular teapot; three bulb bottom mugs with applied handles -- brown (10), ivory (9), and orange. Bottom, left to right: 3¾" mug, bulb bottom with metal clip bakelite handle (10), used as tumbler without clip (same shape as mugs shown having applied handles); creamer; sauce boat (10); stacked 5½" fruit (U); 6½" plate; 7½" plate; demitasse cup (U) and saucer; round-handled creamer.

The Modern California pattern is characterized by its satin-finish soft pastels. A 1938 *Sunset* magazine ad specified color choices of azure (blue), pistachio (green), straw (yellow), and orchid. Additional colors described in an earlier September 1937 ad are gray and beige. Pictured are a few items to be found in Modern California. All have mark 14 except as noted. Notice the rounded shapes here compared to the angular shape in Early California.

Top, left to right:
Pistachio coffee server, matching bakelite handle (the coffee server is interchangeable with most shapes); 9½" plate; 12½" platter; 10" vegetable; 9½" comport (scarce).

Center, left to right:
Cup; saucer; muffin tray and cover; early mug with clip bakelite handle (10); sauce boat; teapot; demitasse cup (U) and saucer; and applied handled mug.

Bottom, left to right:
Covered lug chowder; 3" ash tray.

In addition to the two styles of mugs described in these photos, another early shape was produced which resembles an elongated flower pot, having a raised upper rim and wider base rim. Still another corset shaped 4" mug with clip handle was produced in 1937 but an example was not available for photographing.

Beginning in the mid 1930's, colorful hand painted patterns were executed on the Montecito shape. Most patterns were named; a few were identified only by number and some had both number and name. A number preceded by "T" evidently indicated a Turnbull design.

The Native American design was featured in the "Window Shopping" column of *House Beautiful*, December 1937 issue. The ad stated, "From California and the Vernon Kilns of California comes this essentially native product, very aptly called 'Native American'. Gale Turnbull, its designer, is inspired by the carefree existence of California in old Mission days. There are ten designs and you can buy mixed or all alike..." The designs depicted people in native dress, missions and little mission houses, cacti and scenes in old California. The ad pictured the coffee server with Pedro and Conchita, and two plates, one the same as in the photo on page 68, the other a house with Pedro and Conchita standing before it. The coffee server was priced at $3.00, 7" plates at 60 cents each, and a 22-piece set for $9.50. What a bargain for hand-painted ware!

Casa California (translated California Home) patterns feature a group of colorful, handpainted florals in blues and greens (T-631) and zinnia tones of browns and yellows (T-630 and T-632), all on cream background. Described in 1938 ads as being the "modern adaptation of a primitive peasant decoration" and "new peasant patterns designed by Gale Turnbull for Vernon Kilns." Even the company's gift boxes, containing 45-piece plate settings, were decorated with Turnbull's distinctive art, a scene of a mission, mountain and cacti.

The next three photos feature Turnbull patterns, believed to date in the 1936-1939 period.

Simple designs having pattern name or number, mark 33, exceptions are noted. Top, left to right: Blend No. 10, 9½" plate; T-659, 10½" plate; Blend No. 4, 9½" plate. Bottom, left to right: Blend No. 10 cup and saucer (33, initials only); Blend No. 4, 4½" tumbler (has matching 1 quart bulbous bottom pitcher); T-652 8½" plate; Blue Star* individual creamer (19); unidentified Blend* regular size creamer with lid.
*Name by author in lieu of company name or number.

Scenic Coastline and **Native American** series -- all marked 33 except as noted. Top: Banana Tree coffee server. Center, left to right: Coastline 9½'' plate (map from Santa Barbara to San Diego, California); Michigan Coastline 12'' chop plate (map of lake and surrounding cities, Chicago and Grand Rapids); Coastline 10½'' plate a map of California coast from San Francisco to San Luis Obispo (19). Bottom, left to right: Native American designs -- Little Mission 9'' vegetable; Pedro & Conchita 7½'' plate; Cottage Window 9'' vegetable (may not be one of the Native American designs).

Top, left to right: T-631 8'' mixing bowl, one of a nest of five; T-632 12'' chop plate; T-631 9½'' plate (33). Bottom, left to right: T-630 muffin tray and cover; T-630 9½'' plate; and a bulb bottom pitcher (10) pattern not known and NOT Casa California though somewhat similar pattern and believed to be a Turnbull design.

About the same time the **Native American** series was introduced, the "plaids" made their debut executed on the Montecito shape. The first "plaids" designed by Gale Turnbull were grouped under the name Organdie. In 1937, an ad for Organdie describes it as the "bold, gay patterns of crisp organdie, subdued and mellowed by undertones of contrasting color and design". The ad informs that the "plaid" patterns were painted by hand under the glaze, each piece signed by Mr. Turnbull, and came in a variety of gay, attractive colors on a neutral background, but colors were not given. Another ad, however, pictured Coronation Organdy (note different spelling of "organdy"), stating that colors were gray and rose; still another ad in *Homes of the West*, September 1937 described colors in "two-tone combinations of green, brown, blue and pink-and-gray". Early Organdie patterns have been found numbered T-508, grey and rose (Coronation Organdy);T-511, brown and yellow; T-512, deep rose and green; T-513, pale yellow and green. The Coronation Organdy ad listed a coffee server at $2.95 and a muffin dish at $2.25. These first "plaids" were the forerunners of the six popular "plaids" of the 1940's and 1950's: Organdie, Homespun, Tam O'Shanter, Gingham, Calico and Tweed, one of Vernon's most popular pattern groups of all time. Sometimes the hand-painted patterns were sold in combination with the bold colors of Early California or subdued pastels of Modern California.

Another long time favorite, handpainted Brown Eyed Susan, may have been first introduced as early as 1940 since a few pieces have been found on the Ultra shape.

Group of handpainted patterns, including "plaids" and a transfer print in two different colors. All have mark 19 except as noted.

Top, left to right: Blossoms T-704, 10½" plate; T-638, 9½" plate (both 33). 2nd row, left to right: Victoria 9½" plate (16); Linda 836, 14" chop plate; 707, 14½" platter. 3rd row, left to right: 707 teapot; Gingham 10½" platter (21); Dainty sugar without lid (16), same as Victoria but rose-colored print. A third identical pattern, Trailing Rose, is blue, but was not available for photographing. Bottom, left to right: Meadow Bloom creamer (21); 707, 8½" platter; Organdie spoon holder (21); ceramic card-holder dealer sign (U); Mexicana creamer and saucer (21).

An assortment of "plaids" along with a couple of scarce Brown Eyed Susan items, marked 22 unless noted.

Top, left to right:
Brown Eyed Susan 4" pepper mill, scarce (U); Gingham 1 pint bowl; Calico large pepper shaker (U), shown on Calico saucer (21).

Center, left to right:
Organdie 8" covered casserole (actually measures 11" including handles, 8" is inside diameter. 8" is size listed in company price lists); Tam O'Shanter 11½" double vegetable (21); Organdie T-512 saucer (33, initials only); Brown Eyed Susan 3" regular size salt shaker (U); Tweed wood handle 14" serving tray (21).

Bottom, left to right:
Organdie saucer candleholder with aluminum fittings (base covers mark); Organdie butter tray and cover; Brown Eyed Susan saucer candleholder with brass fittings (base covers mark). Both candleholders are scarce. Candlesticks were also made from tea cups with brass fittings. A chandelier utilizing tea cups has been reported.

More examples of the Montecito shape to be found in "plaids" and Brown Eyed Susan. All marked 21 unless noted.

Top, left to right:
Organdie creamer (22) -- note difference in spout compared to Meadow Bloom creamer; Brown Eyed Susan sugar bowl (22); Organdie 10½" salad bowl -- individual 5½" salad bowls with straight sides were made to go with the large bowl but no examples were available for photographing.

Center, left to right:
Gingham 7½" round vegetable; Brown Eyed Susan sauce boat (22); 10" oval vegetable; Organdie No. 513, 9½" plate (33); Brown Eyed Susan #838, 9½" plate, Ultra shape, rare (19).

Bottom, left to right:
Tam O'Shanter chowder; Homespun butter pat or lapel pin (marked Vernonware, Calif. U.S.A. only); Brown Eyed Susan 9" round vegetable; Tam O'Shanter 4" coaster; Organdie 8½" rim soup.

Here are examples of Montecito earlier shapes compared to later shapes in popular patterns. Earlier pitcher shapes are bulbous and the later are streamline. Double egg cups were the cupped-in style and later styles had slanted sides. Early tumblers had a flared rim and later styles were convex-sided. All are marked 22 except where noted.

Top, left to right:
Tweed drip-cut top syrup pitcher (21) -- plaid syrups were listed in 1954 at $3.75 and 1956 at $4.00; Brown Eyed Susan 9 oz. 3½" coffee mug; Organdie coffee server (not original stopper).

Center, left to right:
707, 13 oz. iced tea; Homespun 1 pint pitcher, bulbous style; Brown Eyed Susan double egg cup (U); Organdie 4" flower pot with matching saucer; Tam O'Shanter 2 quart ice-lip pitcher, streamlined (21).

Bottom, left to right:
707 double egg cup (U); Gingham individual 4" covered stick-handle chicken pie server; Organdie stick-handle batter bowl (U) -- this is not shown in any available company price lists and may be a Metlox piece; ½ pint Gingham streamline pitcher. January 1954 price list showed five sizes of these pitchers; Homespun 14 oz. tumbler.

Three sizes of cups and saucers are pictured. A fourth, the jumbo size, which consisted of a cup 4¼ "in diameter and a 6¾ " saucer, was not available for photographing.

The Tam O'Shanter Colossal cup (27) is a 4 quart version of the tea cup. A January 1953 price list stated "ideal as a collector's item, or for display, salad, punch, fruit, popcorn, planting and flower arrangements." It was also pictured in a company brochure as an ice bucket. The cup measures 9 3/8" and is 5 7/8" deep, the saucer measures 15". The Colossal cup and saucer is considered scarce and was made in only a few patterns for a brief period in the 1950's. The other two, Organdie tea cup and saucer and Homespun demitasse cup and saucer, are shown for size comparison. These are both marked 21 on the saucers only. In June 1955 the Colossal cup and saucer was the most expensive item in its pattern at $12.95, compared to a tea cup and saucer at $1.75.

In 1950, the Winchester '73 pattern was designed by Vernon Kilns. Heisey Glass Company of Newark, Ohio, matched it with their etched bar glassware, also called Winchester '73. The dinnerware and stemware were tied in with the promotion and introduced simultaneously with Universal International's motion picture, *Winchester '73*, starring James Stewart and Shelley Winters. The movie opened at the Paramount Theatre in New York on June 7, 1950 and was released throughout the country during July, August and September of that year. Theatres eagerly wanted to show what stores handled the Winchester '73 pattern in their respective areas. A company brochure described the pattern, "all the romance of the winning of the West is in this attractive new pattern...designed with a particular eye to masculine taste...for casual dining anytime, anywhere. Winchester '73 has he-man appeal with its bold Western scenes, cowboys, covered wagons...in dramatic colors on a soft green background." (It has been noted that Winchester '73 has a creamy background while Frontier Days has a soft green color.) Faye Bennison, Vernon Kilns founder and owner, informed the writer that the design had originally been made for 500 coffee mugs presented to employees and guests at a Winchester Arms convention. None of these has been found and perhaps it is identical to the mug sold with the set, or possibly it was personalized. By January 1953 the pattern name was changed to Frontier Days due to a conflict with the Winchester Arms company over use of their name. Paul Davidson did the artwork and almost every piece carries his signature, sometimes humorously obscured in the artwork. For example, the vegetable bowl pictures the Davidson's saloon with its proprietor, P. L. Davidson. Collectors will be delighted to learn this pattern has many extra pieces.

Winchester '73 or Frontier Days, Montecito shape.

Top, left to right: 14" chop plate (42) 10½" dinner plate; cup and saucer (42). Bottom, left to right: 9" round vegetable; 6½" plate; 10" oval platter; covered creamer; 7½" plate (42).

Coronado Shape (a variation of Montecito)

This solid color pattern named Coronado was available as premium ware in 1938 and 1939. In the eastern states it reportedly was obtained through gas stations. In Southern California it was offered at a major supermarket chain and, as pictured in the *Sunset* magazine ad of April 1938, was available with a label from Lynden Chicken Fricassee. As stated in the ad, colors were blue (dark), orange, green, turquoise and yellow. In addition, pink, light blue and brown have been found. Much of this ware is unmarked, but when marked, 10 or 11 are most common. As shown in the photo it is easily recognized by its angular handles and the "cubist" band about half an inch below rims of holloware and on the rims of flatware and tumblers. A shape with round handles and the "cubist" band at the base of holloware is believed to be a variation of Coronado. Cups in this variation have a wider base. It is not known how many Coronado items were made. This shape was also used for the Mexicana motif.

All Coronado items pictured are unmarked except as noted. Sometimes they are marked only "Made in U.S.A."

Top, left to right:
12½" oval platter; sugar bowl with "cubist" band at base; 9" vegetable (10).

Center, left to right:
Coffee server, the "cubist" band encircles middle; 6½" plate (11); saucer (11); cup (10); tumbler; 7½" flat rim soup (10); two 6½" plates.

Bottom, left to right:
Creamer (10); cup with "cubist" band at base; 5½" fruit; creamer (variation).

A full page color ad from the April 1938 issue of *Sunset* magazine. Lynden Chicken Fricassee was offering Coronado dinnerware for $1.00 and a label from the can.

The following are all known patterns on the Montecito shape.

Name/Number	Description	Approx. Date of Production	Artist
After Glow	Solid yellow combined with ivory bottom and interior.	1935-1937	Bird
Banana Tree	Handpainted tree, ivory background. Believed to be in Native American series.	1937	Turnbull
Beige	Allover solid beige.	1935-1937	Bird
Blend #4	Handpainted mustard to green blend of concentric rings.	1938	Turnbull
Blend #10	Handpainted pink to green blend of concentric rings.	1938	Turnbull
Blossoms T-704	Handpainted border of scattered blue blossoms. Cream background.	1937	Turnbull
Blue Star (name by author	Tiny blue stars on blue background. Until company name is known, this name is given to identify.	1938	Turnbull
Brown Eyed Susan*	Perky yellow daisies, green leaves on ivory background. Meadow Bloom same except for colors.	1946-1958	
B-156	Blue floral, yellow background.	1935-1937	Bird
B-300	Geometric border design. Orange and green ¼″ dots spaced and separated by narrow wavy yellow line encircling the flat rim. Ivory background. Possibly one of the Spectrum series.	1935-1937	Bird
B-305	Bright green tubular flowers with yellow stamens connected by curving line encircling border.	1935-1937	Bird
B-310	Multicolor geometric triangular border, ivory background. Spectrum series.	1935-1937	Bird
B-327	Polychromatic stylized petal outline on ivory background. Same as Multi Flori California except for color.	1935-1937	Bird
BB-2	Colorful floral, wide blue rim, ivory background	1935-1937	Bird
Calico	Handpainted pink and blue plaid, one of the "plaid" group	1949-1954 Special order 1955	
Casa California	See T-630, T-631, T-632.		
Coastline	Handpainted outline of Pacific Coast map. Blue, black on ivory background.	1937	Turnbull
Coronado	(Montecito variation). Solid colors: dark blue, brown, yellow, orange, blue, turquoise, pink and light green.	1935-1939	

Name/Number	Description	Approx. Date of Production	Artist
Coronation Organdy	Gray and rose plaid. Also T-508	1937	Turnbull
Cottage Window	Handpainted curtained window, provincial style. Believed to be Native American series.	1937	Turnbull
Country Side	New England type rural scene. Rolling hills, fenced farm houses and barns, steepled church. Touches of red of roofs, green leaves. Green transfer on ivory background. This pattern is unmarked Vernon Kilns. The backstamp carries the name of da Bron, along with pattern name. Handpainted under glaze. Made in California.	1950	Davidson
Dainty	Tiny leaves and flowers. All-over transfer, deep pink hand-tinted print. Trailing Rose and Victoria same pattern, different colors.	1939	
Early California	Solid colors: Pre-1946, orange, dark blue, pink, brown, turquoise, blue, ivory, green, maroon. 1946, green, blue, peach, turquoise, and yellow.	1935-1947	
Evening Star	One of the solid group, blue combined with ivory interiors or bottomsides.	1935-1937	Bird
Frontier Days (or Winchester '73)	Transfer of Western scenes, hand-tinted brown print, soft green background.	1950 Special order 1954	Davidson
Gingham	Handpainted green and yellow plaid with green border. One of the "plaid" group.	1949-1958	
Golden Maple	One of the solid group, pumpkin combined with ivory interiors or bottomsides.	1935-1937	Bird
Homespun*	Handpainted green, rust, and yellow plaid with rust border. One of the "plaid" group.	1949-1958	
Linda #836	Handpainted blue and maroon floral on ivory background, maroon rim.	1940	
Little Mission	Handpainted scene of mission house. Native American series.	1937	Turnbull
Marines	Nautical motif of anchor and ships.	1937	Turnbull
Meadow Bloom	Handpainted rose and blue flowers, brown shaded border. Same as Brown Eyed Susan, different colors.	1947	

Name/Number	Description	Approx. Date of Production	Artist
Mexicana	Handpainted bands of color on border, deep yellow, rust to dark brown. Not to be confused with Mexicana scene decal of early 1930 period.	1950 Special order 1954	
Michigan Coastline	Handpainted outline of Lake Michigan coastline, in blue and black on ivory.	1937	Turnbull
Milkweed Dance	(Montecito and Ultra.) All-over floral, leaf transfer in two colors, blue or maroon print.	1940	Disney
Modern California	Solid colors: 1937, azure, orchid, pistachio, straw, sand and gray. Ivory also produced.	1937-1947	
Montecito	Early pattern name.	1935	
Multi Flori California	Monochromatic stylized petal outline in green, brown, blue, yellow or rose on ivory background. Same as B-327 except single color.	1935-1937	Bird
Native American	Series which includes: Little Mission, Pedro & Conchita, Banana Tree and perhaps Cottage Window.	1935-1937	Turnbull
North Wind	Handpainted two color combination, wide outer dark green band, center lime green.	1948	
Olinala-Aztec	Authentic Aztec design of floral and geometric band. Soft blue, green, yellow or rose on warm beige (ivory) background. Hand inlaid glaze.	1937	Bird
Organdie*	Handpainted brown and yellow plaid. One of the "plaid" group.	1940-1958	Turnbull
Organdie 511	Handpainted brown and yellow plaid.	1937	Turnbull
Organdie T-512	Handpainted deep rose and green.		
Organdie 513	Handpainted yellow and green. This is the first group of plaids.		
Organdy (Coronation)	See T-508		
Pedro & Conchita	Handpainted scene of man and woman in native dress. Native American series.	1937	Turnbull
Plaids	See Calico, Gingham, Homespun, Organdie, Tam O'Shanter and Tweed.		
Polychrome A	Inlaid glaze. Bright varied colored blocks resembling tiles decorate rims. Possibly one of the Spectrum designs.	1935-1937	Bird
Pomegranate	One of the solid color group. Solid bright pink combined with ivory interiors and bottomsides.	1935-1937	Bird

Name/Number	Description	Approx. Date of Production	Artist
Spice Islands	Sailing ships, spices surround map and words "East Indies and West Indies". Touches of blue, yellow and brown on brown transfer, ivory background. Pattern is unmarked Vernon Kilns. Backstamp carries name of da Bron, pattern name, Handpainted Under Glaze, Made in California.	1950	Davidson
Tam O'Shanter	Rust, chartreuse, green plaid with green border. One of the "plaid" group.	1949-1958	
Trailing Rose	Transfer. Tiny leaves and flowers, all-over blue or red print on ivory. Same as Dainty and Victory except for color.	1939	
Tweed	Handpainted gray and yellow plaid. One of the "plaids".	1950-1954 Special Order 1955	
Two-Some T-698	Two wide brown shaded bands on rim, cream background.	1938	Turnbull
T-508	Handpainted rose and grey plaid.	1937	Turnbull
T-511	See Organdie		
T-512	See Organdie		
T-513	See Organdie		
T-630	Casa California. Handpainted provincial peasant floral design in browns and yellows, cream background.	1938	Turnbull
T-631	Casa California. Handpainted vase and flowers in blues and greens, cream background.	1938	Turnbull
T-632	Casa California. Handpainted provincial floral in browns and yellows, cream background.	1938	Turnbull
T-6____	Casa California. Handpainted provincial floral in blues and greens, cream background, same as T-632 except for color. Number is not known, but is probably 633.	1938	Turnbull
T-638	Two color bands, shaded yellow and blue, on rim.	1937	Turnbull
T-652	Handpainted blue feather on solid blue background.	1938	Turnbull
T-653	Handpainted wide bands of pink and mauve on rim surround orchid floral on pale yellow center.	1938	Turnbull
T-654	Handpainted mauve rim, lavender floral on pale mauve background.	1938	Turnbull

Name/Number	Description	Approx. Date of Production	Artist
T-657	Fleur-de-lis handpainted design. Ivory feathers, blue bow, pink background, wide ivory border.	1938	Turnbull
T-659	Handpainted blue bow on narrow blue banded rim. Solid blue background.	1938	Turnbull
T-698 Two-Some	See Two-Some.		
T-704	See Blossoms.		
Victoria	Transfer. Tiny leaves and flowers all over hand-tinted green print. Same as Dainty, Trailing Rose, except for color.	1939	
Winchester '73	See Frontier Days. Same, except Winchester '73 background is usually cream.	1950	Davidson
707	Handpainted elaborate floral, yellow rims.	1940	
836	See Linda.		

*Metlox continued pattern for a short time.

Prices For Montecito and Coronado

Coronado is included here for value--only a few items will be found on the Coronado shape. All items will not be found in all patterns. Solid colors orange, dark blue, brown and lavender will have a higher value.

Ash Trays, 3″ square 4.00- 8.00
    4″ round (coaster) 5.00- 9.00
    5½″ round 6.00-11.00
Bowls, 5½″ fruit 4.00- 8.00
    *5½″ salad, individual 6.00-10.00
    6″ lug chowder, covered 10.00-15.00
    6″ lug chowder, open 6.00-12.00
    8½″ rim soup 6.00-12.00
    8½″ coupe soup (Mexicana only) 6.00-12.00
    7½″ serving, round 6.00-9.00
    8½″ serving, round 7.00-10.00
    9″ serving, round or oval 8.00-12.00
    10″ serving, oval 8.00-12.00
    10″ divided serving, oval 10.00-15.00
    *10½″ salad 12.00-22.00
    13″ serving, round, (early) 20.00-45.00
    1 pint 6.00-12.00
Mixing, 4-piece set
Mixing, 5-piece set
    5″ 5.00-7.00
    6″ 6.00-9.00

7″	7.00-11.00
8″	8.00-13.00
9″	9.00-15.00
*Butter pat, 2½″, individual	5.00- 9.00
Butter tray, covered, oblong	10.00-35.00
*Candleholder, saucer, metal fitting	15.00-18.00
Casserole, covered, 8″ (inside diameter), oven	30.00-35.00
*4″ individual, covered	12.00-18.00
*4″ chicken pie, covered, stick handle	12.00-18.00
*"Casserole Hot", black wrought iron stand, candle warmer	12.00-18.00
*"Casserole Round-Up", black wrought iron stand, candle warmer	20.00-25.00
Coaster, 4″ round (same as ash tray)	5.00- 9.00
Coffee Pot, 7″, 2-cup, after dinner, rare	35.00-50.00
Coffee server (carafe) and stopper, 10-cup	14.00-25.00
stopper only	4.00- 8.00
*"Coffee Hot", black wrought iron stand with candle warmer	12.00-18.00
Creamer, open, individual	6.00-12.00
open, regular	6.00-11.00
covered, regular	10.00-18.00
Comport, 9½″, rare (Early & Modern Calif. only)	20.00-35.00
Cups, custard, 3″, rare	12.00-22.00
Cups and saucers, After Dinner cup, 2 7/8″	10.00-15.00
saucer, 5¼″	2.00- 4.00
tea cup, 4″	8.00-15.00
saucer, 6½″	2.00-4.00
*jumbo cup, 4¼″, 12 oz.	12.00-20.00
saucer, 6¾″	3.00- 5.00
*colossal cup, 9 3/8″, 4 quart	30.00-50.00
saucer, 15″	10.00-15.00
Egg cup, double	8.00-15.00
Flower Pots, *3″	10.00-15.00
saucer	5.00- 6.00
*4″	12.00-20.00
saucer	6.00-8.00
*5″	15.00-25.00
saucer	7.00-10.00
Jam jar, 5″, notched lid	30.00-45.00
lid only	7.00-10.00
Lemon server, 6″, center handle	15.00-20.00
Muffin tray, 9″, tab handles, dome cover	30.00-45.00
cover only	12.00-22.00
Mugs, 3¾″ bulb bottom, 8 oz., clip handle (early version)	10.00-18.00
3¾″ bulb bottom, 8 oz., applied handle (early version)	12.00-22.00
3½″ straight sided, 9 oz. (later version)	10.00-18.00
Pitchers, disk, 2 quart (early)	16.00-30.00
jug, 1 pint	8.00-15.00
1 quart	12.00-18.00
streamlined, *¼ pint	6.00-10.00

*½ pint	8.00-12.00
1 pint	10.00-15.00
1 quart	12.00-20.00
2 quart	15.00-25.00
*syrup, drip-cut top	35.00-45.00
tankard (early), scarce	20.00-35.00
Plates, *2½ " lapel plate with pin	15.00-25.00
4¼ " miniature (coaster)	5.00- 7.00
6½ " bread & butter	3.00- 6.00 **
7½ " salad	4.00-8.00 **
9½ " luncheon	6.00-12.00 **
10½ " dinner	8.00-15.00 **
11 " grill (early)	10.00-18.00
12 " chop	12.00-20.00 **
13 " chop	13.00-22.00 **
14 " chop	14.00-25.00 **
16½ "-17 " chop	20.00-35.00 **
Two-tier	10.00-18.00
Three-tier	12.00-20.00
Platters, 8½ " (relish)	7.00-10.00
9½ "	8.00-12.00
10½ "	10.00-15.00
12 "	12.00-18.00
14 "	14.00-20.00
16 "	16.00-35.00
Relish, 7x10, clover shape, 3 part	25.00-35.00
Sauce boat, (gravy)	10.00-18.00
double spout, with attached underplate (early)	12.00-22.00
Shakers, salt, regular	4.00- 8.00
*salt, large (also listed as salt cellar)	5.00- 9.00
pepper, regular	4.00- 8.00
*pepper, large	5.00- 9.00
*pepper mill (large shaker with metal fitting)	20.00-35.00
*Spoon holder	12.00-20.00
Sugar, covered, individual	10.00-15.00
covered, regular	6.00-12.00
Teapot, covered, 8-cup, round	18.00-35.00
6-cup, angular	20.00-45.00
Tumblers, 3¾ " bulb bottom, 8 oz. (early)	10.00-18.00
4 " Coronado, 8 oz.	10.00-18.00
4¼ " raised upper rim, wide base rim (early)	12.00-22.00
4½ " concave sides, 13 oz.	12.00-22.00
5 " convex sides, 14 oz.	12.00-22.00

*Items made in the 1950's only in popular patterns: Brown Eyed Susan, Gingham, Homespun, Mexicana, Organdie, Tam O'Shanter, Tweed, and Calico.
**Double the higher value for decorator and hanging plates in these patterns:

Banana Tree	Little Mission	Pedro & Conchita
B-156	Milkweed Dance	Winchester '73 (Frontier Days)
Cottage Window	Olinala-Aztec	

Ultra Shape

This overall shape is credited to Gale Turnbull, the "upside-down" handles of the holloware to Jane Bennison. The shape was used chiefly for the designer patterns of Rockwell Kent, Don Blanding, Walt Disney, (though some Disney patterns were executed on a combination of Ultra flatware and Montecito holloware), and Turnbull's own designs. The ware is distinctive for the narrow "dipped" rims on coupe-shaped flatware and the "upside-down" handles. This shape is believed to have been discontinued in the early 1940's. The photographs show all available examples of items and patterns in the Ultra shape beginning with the Ultra California pattern.

Ultra California was the name given to the solid color pattern. The name Ultra is used to identify the shape as well because the company name for the shape is not known. A November 1939 *House Beautiful* ad described the colors as rich half-tones in buttercup (yellow), gardenia (ivory), carnation (pink), and aster (blue). Other colors which have been found are maroon (rare), and ice green. All items pictured have mark 15.

Top, left to right:
2 quart disk jug (interchangeable with other shapes); 8½" plate; 13 oz. iced tea (also interchangeable); 12½" platter; 9½" plate; 6½" plate; 2 cup demitasse pot; 2 quart open pitcher.

Center, left to right:
2-handled covered 8" (inside diameter) casserole; gravy; regular size tea cup and saucer; demitasse cup and saucer; jam jar with notched lid; single egg cup.

Bottom, left to right:
Salt shaker; creamer #1 shape; 5½" fruit; creamer #2 shape. Notice difference in height of two creamers.

84

Simpler handpainted patterns of the Ultra shape are illustrated here. The Rio group and its counterpart Sierra Madre Two-Tone are featured, along with Yellow Rose #1 and #2 and Orchard. All have mark 19 with respective pattern name unless noted.

Top, left to right: T-743 (Yellow Rose #2) teapot (33); Rio Vista 4½″ jam jar with notched lid; Rio Chico 12½″ platter; Sierra Madre Two-Tone 10½″ plate. Center, left to right: T-742 (Yellow Rose #1) sugar bowl (33) -- T-742 and T-743 are the same except for rim color; Orchard 9½″ plate; Rio Vista 8½″ coupe soup; T-742 creamer (33); Rio Verde 7½″ plate. Bottom, left to right: Rio Chico chowder; Rio Vista salt shaker; individual creamer and sugar -- note individual sugar is handleless in the Ultra shape. The difference in the three Rio patterns is in the color of the wide band. Sierra Madre Two-Tone has same colored border (both blue and green are known) but without floral design and can be mixed or matched.

These are the elaborate and beautiful handpainted designs of Gale Turnbull, all with mark 33 except where noted.

Top, left to right: Vera 10-cup coffee pot; Flora 13½″ chop plate; Harvest 1 pint open pitcher (19). Center, left to right: Bouquet 12½″ chop plate; Five Fingers 7½″ plate; Flora 13 oz. ice tea; Harvest 8½″ plate (19). Bottom, left to right: Flora 2 cup demitasse pot; Harvest salt shaker; Vera butter lid only.

Examples of "print and fill" (handpainted). Notice four are the same design but different colors. All are marked 16 except as noted.

Top, left to right: Santa Rose 12½" chop plate; Santa Maria 9½" plate. Bottom, left to right: Taste cup and saucer (34); Santa Paula salt shaker; Santa Barbara 6½" plate; Floret cup and saucer.

Don Blanding's tropical designs were basically three transfer prints and one free handpainted, all executed on Ultra. The colors in the transfer prints determined the pattern name. They are grouped according to design and colors known, as follows. All are on a cream background. There are possibly other colors.

1. Lotus floral:	Hawaiian Flowers	- plain print in different colors of pink, blue, maroon or mustard.
	Honolulu	- hand-tinted yellow flowers on blue print. This same color hand-tinted blue print has been found with the Hawaiian Flowers backstamp as well. It may have been mismarked.
	Hilo	- hand-tinted light brown print.
	Lei Lani	- hand-tinted maroon print. In 1947 this same pattern was executed on San Marino shape.
	Hawaii	- listed here but is the Lei Lani color on Melinda shape about 1942-46.
2. Peony and gardenia: floral:	Glamour	- plain print in blue or maroon.
	Joy	- hand-tinted yellow peony on light brown print.
	Delight	- hand-tinted yellow flowers on blue print.
	Ecstasy	- hand-tinted pink peony, green leaves on light brown print.
3. Tropical Fish:	Coral Reef	- plain print in blue, maroon or mustard.
4. Aquarium		The hand-painted design of Tropical Fish was different on each item and in brilliant colors.

Blanding's mark 35 does not include "handpainted" for the hand-tinted prints, unlike the backstamp for Vernon Kilns other hand-tinted prints. Handpainted Aquarium has the words "handpainted under glaze" added to the mark 35.

Here are examples of the Group 1 design, all bearing mark 35 and respective pattern name, except where noted.

Top, left to right:
Hawaiian Flowers tureenette with notched lid, 7½″ diameter excluding handles (scarce item in any Ultra pattern); Hilo 9½″ plate; Lei Lani coffee pot.

Center, left to right:
Hawaiian Flowers individual sugar; Hawaiian Flowers 13 oz. ice tea tumbler; Hawaiian Flowers 6½″ plate; Lei Lani regular size creamer; Honolulu cup and saucer.

Bottom, left to right:
Hilo individual creamer; Lei Lani butter tray* and cover; Lei Lani lug chowder; Lei Lani salt shaker*; Hawaiian Flowers 8 oz. handled mug*; Hawaiian Flowers demitasse cup and saucer.

A maroon Hawaiian Flowers 15″ console bowl (Bennison Dayrae shape) and sphere candlesticks have been reported. It has been reported that Lei Lani (in blue!) was featured on page 135 of a *Heinz Wartime Supplement Cookbook*, still on the Ultra shape.

*Butter tray and salt shaker backstamp does not include pattern name. Mug is marked only "Vernon Kilns, U.S.A."

Shown are examples of Groups 2 and 3 prints and handpainted Aquarium (Group 4) pattern. All have mark 35. Aquarium also marked "handpainted".

Top, left to right:
Delight 6 cup tea pot; Joy 6½″ plate.
Center, left to right: Aquarium handpainted 6½″ plate; Coral Reef 7½″ plate; Glamour 9½″ plate; Aquarium 13 oz. ice tea tumbler; Ecstasy 7½″ plate.
Bottom, left to right:
Aquarium chowder; Aquarium cup and saucer; Coral Reef 5½″ fruit; Aquarium 7½″ plate.

Through the effort of Mr. Bennison, Rockwell Kent was the second American artist to be hired by Vernon Kilns and he worked from his New York studio. Mr. Bennison visited Rockwell Kent in his New York City studio in the late 1930's and told him of the earlier success of Don Blanding, convincing him of the opportunity to be had working for Vernon Kilns.

Rockwell Kent designed three major dinnerware patterns, all on the Ultra shape: Our America, Moby Dick, and Salamina. Today the plates hold the greatest value for collectors because they are suitable for hanging.

In Our America, Kent drew over thirty designs representing scenes and activities of regions of America. These were transfers in four different colors of print: walnut brown, dark blue, maroon, and green on a cream background. The key piece of the series is a 17¼″ chop plate which features at top center the national Eagle above the American shield, with the eagle's wings outspread over a city on the left, farmlands to the right. Below this grouping is an outline map of the United States with small drawings in perspective, typical of each state or region.

For illustrative purposes, Rockwell Kent considered America as being divided into eight geographical regions as follows: (from an original company brochure "What you will see in Our America").

"No. 1 - New England States: Maine, New Hampshire, Vermont, Connecticut, Massachusetts, Rhode Island
No. 2 - Middle Atlantic States: New York, New Jersey, Pennsylvania, Maryland, Delaware

No. 3 - Southern Colonial States: Virginia, West Virginia, the Carolinas, Georgia
No. 4 - Mississippi River States: Louisiana, Mississippi, Arkansas, Tennessee, Kentucky, Missouri
No. 5 - Great Lakes States: Ohio, Indiana, Illinois, Michigan, Wisconsin, Minnesota
No. 6 - Plains and Mountain States: Texas, Oklahoma, Kansas, Nebraska, the Dakotas, Iowa, Montana, Wyoming, Colorado, New Mexico, Arizona, Utah, Idaho, Nevada
No. 7 - Gulf States: Florida, Alabama
No. 8 - Pacific States: California, Oregon, Washington"

Each piece of flatware was decorated in addition to the star-spangled border, with a central drawing illustrative of one of these eight regions, as follows:

"17" Chop Plate - Map of the United States, described above.

14" Chop Plate - Region No. 8: Across a lake bordered with California Big Trees we see a dam; behind it rise the mountain peaks.

12" Chop Plate - Region No. 6: The rich Middle West corn belt is represented by fields of grain and grain elevators; cattle in the middle distance.

10½" Plate - Region No. 2: New York City seen from the Bay; its outflung piers radiate in the water, its tall buildings reach into a twilight sky.

9½" Plate - Region No. 5: We are approaching Chicago on the River, the drawbridge rises before us; and we see in the distance the buildings of the city.

8½" Plate - Region No. 1: New England's fishing industries are depicted in a busy scene on the fishing banks.

7½" Plate - Region No. 3: The Deep South's romantic past and industrious present combine, with cotton pickers shown before a gracious Colonial mansion.

7½" Soups - Region No. 3: Same picture as 7½" plates.

6½" Plate (and Saucers) - Region No. 4: A stern-wheeler on the Mississippi, taking on a cargo of cotton.

Chowder Bowl - Region No. 7: Coconut palms in Florida, bordering the lagoon."

The holloware was decorated with stars on handles, shoulders, covers and knobs, and illustrations on the sides of holloware pieces were as follows:

"Tea Cups - Region No. 4: Incoming and outgoing freight crowds the wharves at New Orleans.

After Dinner Cups - Region No. 1: Yacht racing at Newport.

After Dinner Saucers - Same as After Dinner Cups.

Pickle Dish - Same as After Dinner Cups and Saucers.

Jumbo Cups - Region No. 1: Tapping the trees for maple sugar in the snowy Vermont winter.

Jumbo Saucers - Same as Jumbo Cups.

Regular Sugar Bowl - Region No. 4: Workers cutting waving fields of sugar cane.

Regular Creamer - Region No. 7: The floating homes of houseboaters in Florida.

Individual Sugar - Region No. 4: Shrimp fisherman plying their trade in the Gulf of Mexico.

Individual Creamer - Region No. 7: Scene in the wilds of the Florida Everglades.

Casserole - Region No. 5: Steamers and yachts on the Great Lakes.

Tureenette - Region No. 8: The giant trees in the Northwest fall beneath the lumberman's axes.

2 Quart Pitcher - Region No. 2: To house the workers of the great city, skyscrapers rise.

Teapot - Region No. 6: The picturesque Indians of the high Mesa are shown herding their sheep.

Regular Coffee Pot - Region No. 8: Building one of our great suspension bridges.

Individual Coffee Pot - Region No. 3: A gentleman's sport in a gentleman's state -riding to hounds in Virginia.

Pint Jug - Region No. 8: Steamers on the Columbia River, 4½″ tall.

Mug - Region No. 3: The Blue Grass Country and its blue-blooded stock in the Sport of Kings.

Jam Jar - Region No. 6: Towering oil derricks salute the oil fields of Texas.

13 oz. Tumbler - Region No. 5: Speed boats racing on the Great Lakes.

Butter Dish and Cover - Region No. 4: Steamboat coming around the bend on the lower Mississippi.

Sauce Boat - Region No. 6: Smelters in the mining country.

Egg Cup - Region No. 1: The stately old buildings of a New England college campus stand among the trees.

Muffin Cover - Region No. 1: The fishing fleet puts out to sea.

Salt and Pepper Shakers - Region No. 4: Flat boats on a southern river.

Pint Bowl - Region No. 7: Sailfishing.''

This is Our America dinnerware, each bearing the Rockwell Kent mark 36 unless otherwise noted.

Top, left to right:
10 cup coffee pot (Pacific States, bridge building); cup and saucer (Mississippi River States, New Orleans wharves); 2 quart pitcher (Middle Atlantic States, skyscraper building).

Center:
Regular creamer (Gulf States, houseboaters).

Bottom, left to right:
Sauce boat (Plains and Mountain States, mining country smelters); regular sugar bowl (Mississippi States, sugar cane fields); salt and pepper shakers (Mississippi River States, flat boats on river); casserole (Great Lakes States, boating).

More examples of Our America, all on the Ultra Shape.

Top, left to right: 12″ chop plate (Plains and Mountain States, Middle West grain fields); jam jar base, lid missing, (Plains and Mountain States, Texas oil derricks); 10½″ plate (Middle Atlantic States, New York City); 5½″ fruit (Gulf States, Florida Coconut palms); 14″ chop plate (Pacific States, big trees and lakes, the West). Bottom, left to right: 8½″ plate (New England States, fishing banks); 7½″ plate (Southern Colonial States, cotton pickers, Old South); pickle dish (New England States, yacht racing); 9½″ plate (Great Lakes States, Chicago as seen from the river); 6½″ plate (Mississippi River States, stern-wheeler).

Moby Dick was the most popular Rockwell Kent pattern. The scenes of full-rigged whalers, leaping porpoise and spouting whales were adapted from his illustrations for Herman Melville's classic, *Moby Dick*. It was plain print available in four colors: dark blue, maroon, walnut brown and light orange, each piece bearing Rockwell Kent's signature, Mark 36.

Moby Dick examples on Ultra shape.

Left to right: Single egg cup; salt and pepper shakers; 9½″ plate; 8 oz. handled mug; 1 pint bowl; demitasse cup and saucer; 4″ block candlesticks (rare). These candlesticks have been found in undecorated ivory with the Jane Bennison mark, so the design is attributed to her.

Also known is a 15″ salad bowl (Bennison Dayrae shape) in light orange which is very rare.

91

Salamina also was adapted from a best selling book. Kent's *Salamina*, was the chronicle of his life in Greenland and so named for his housekeeper. Rockwell Kent stated in his book that Salamina was of all the women of North Greenland, the most faithful, noble and most beautiful and most altogether captivating. This was the only Kent design that was handtinted, and is considered the most valuable of all Kent dinnerware.

Examples of Salamina dinnerware, all bearing mark 36 with respective pattern name.

Left to right: Regular size sugar bowl with lid, iceberg scene; cup with same scene; 10½″ plate of Salamina kneeling; 6½″ plate of Salamina peering out over the Arctic waters; tumbler featuring Salamina in native costume holding coffee pot and cup.

Probably the scarcest of the designer dinnerware is Walt Disney's Fantasia line on the Ultra shape. Again transfer prints, some hand-tinted, were two basic floral designs; one an allover pattern, the other a border. Different pattern names were given to each print determined by color or hand-tint. All known patterns* are listed here.

Border:	Enchantment	- hand-tint blue print
	Nutcracker	- hand-tint brown print
	Flower Ballet	- hand-tint maroon print
	Dewdrop Fairies	- plain blue print.
Allover:	Autumn Ballet	- hand-tint maroon print
	Fairyland	- hand-tint blue print
	Milkweed Dance	- two colors have been found in this pattern: plain blue and plain maroon prints
	Fantasia	- hand-tint brown print.

*Also a pattern Firefly has been reported, but description is not known.

Walt Disney dinnerware examples that were available are pictured. All have the Disney backstamp 37 along with respective pattern name.

Top, left to right: Enchantment 10½" plate, Autumn Ballet 14" charger encased in pewter rim; Fairyland 8½" plate. Nymphs are found in the latter two. Bottom, left to right: Nutcracker 6½" plate; Milkweed Dance sugar bowl; Fantasia salt and pepper shakers (sugar bowl and shakers executed on Montecito shape); Flower Ballet tea cup and saucer. On the saucer is a nymph touching a flower with her wand.

Additional dinnerware items reported are a 16½" platter in Milkweed Dance and an Autumn Ballet muffin tray and cover.

Close-up view of Nutcracker teapot, creamer and sugar.

The following are all known patterns on the Ultra shape.

Name/Number	Description	Approx. Date of Production	Artist
Abundance	Transfer border of tiny fruit and floral design. Maroon print. Same as Taste without handtinting.	1939	Turnbull
Aquarium	Handpainted tropical fish, ivory background.	1938	Blanding

Name/Number	Description	Approx. Date of Production	Artist
Autumn Ballet	Allover floral, leaf transfer hand-tinted maroon. Same as Fairyland, Milkweed Dance, Fantasia, in other colors.	1940	Disney
Bouquet	Handpainted elaborate floral, yellow rims.	1938	Turnbull
Brown Eyed Susan #838	Perky yellow daisies, green leaves on ivory background.	possibly 1940	
Coral Reef	Transfer print tropical fish. Blue, mustard or maroon on cream background.	1938	Blanding
Delight	Peony and gardenia transfer, allover blue print, hand-tinted yellow flowers. Glamour, Joy and Ecstasy same pattern, different colors.	1938	Blanding
Dewdrop Fairies	Border transfer, blue print on cream background. Same as Enchantment, Nutcracker, Flower Ballet, different colors.	1940	Disney
Ecstasy	Peony and gardenia transfer, allover hand-tinted light brown print. Delight, Glamour, Joy, same pattern, different colors.	1938	Blanding
Enchantment	Border transfer, hand-tinted blue print. Same as Dewdrop Fairies, Nutcracker and Flower Ballet, different colors.	1940	Disney
Fairyland	All-over floral, leaf transfer hand-tinted blue print. Same as Autumn Ballet, Milkweed Dance, and Fantasia, different colors.	1940	Disney
Fantasia	All-over floral, leaf transfer, hand-tinted brown print. Same as Autumn Ballet, Milkweed Dance and Fairyland, different colors.	1940	Disney
Five Fingers	Handpainted stylized autumn leaves and tendrils on ivory background.	1938	Turnbull
Flora	Handpainted elaborate floral spray.	1938	Turnbull
Floret	Allover floral transfer, hand-tinted red print.	1939	
Flower Ballet	Border transfer, hand-tinted maroon print. Same as Enchantment, Nutcracker, Dewdrop Fairies, different colors.	1940	Disney
Glamour	Peony and gardenia transfer, allover blue or maroon print. Delight, Ecstasy and Joy same pattern, different colors.	1938	Blanding

Name/Number	Description	Approx. Date of Production	Artist
Harvest	Handpainted elaborate design of fruit on ivory background, yellow rims.	1938	Turnbull
Hawaiian Flowers	Lotus transfer, allover pink, blue, maroon or mustard print.	1938	Blanding
Hilo	Transfer lotus flower, allover hand-tinted light brown print.	1938	Blanding
Honolulu	Transfer Lotus flower, allover hand-tinted yellow on blue print.	1938	Blanding
Joy	Peony and gardenia transfer, hand-tinted yellow on brown print. Same pattern as Glamour, Delight, Ecstasy, different colors.	1938	Blanding
Lei Lani (1939-1942)	Lotus transfer, allover hand-tinted maroon print. Hawaii is the same pattern only on the Melinda shape.	1938 Special order 1954-1955	
Milkweed Dance	(Montecito and Ultra). Allover floral, leaf transfer in two colors, blue or maroon print.	1940	Disney
Moby Dick	Transfer whaling scenes. Blue, brown, orange (rare), and maroon print.	1939	Kent
Nutcracker	Border transfer, hand-tinted brown print. Same as Enchantment, Flower Ballet and Dewdrop Fairies except for color.	1940	Disney
Orchard	Handpainted simple fruit design.	1937	Turnbull
Our America	Transfer. Over 30 different scenes of America decorate dinnerware. Colors: brown, blue, maroon, or green print.	1939	Kent
Rio Chico, Rio Verda, Rio Vista	Pink, green, or blue. Identical except for color of border. Hand-painted small floral center.	1938	
Salamina	Transfer, features Greenland scenes and girl, Salamina. Brilliantly hand-tinted print.	1939	Kent
Sierra Madre	Same as Rio group without floral in	1938	
Style	Transfer border of tiny fruit and floral design. Raised handtinted enameling on green print. Same as Taste except different color.	1939	Turnbull
Two-Tone	center. Wide color borders in pink, blue or green. Would combine with Rio patterns.		
Taste	Transfer border of tiny fruit and floral design, hand-tinted maroon print. Same as Abundance and Style, different colors.	1939	Turnbull

Name/Number	Description	Approx. Date of Production	Artist
T-742	Handpainted small yellow rose on cream background, blue rim. Has been called Yellow Rose (#1).	1938	Turnbull
T-743	Same as T-742, except lime green rim. Yellow Rose (#2).	1938	Turnbull
Ultra California	Solid colors: Yellow, ivory, pink, blue, pale green and maroon (rare).	1937-1942	Turnbull
Vera	Handpainted elaborate floral.	1938	Turnbull
838	See Brown Eyed Susan.		

Prices For Ultra

Bowls, 5½" fruit 3.00- 6.00
6" cereal 6.00-12.00
6" chowder, open 6.00-12.00
6" chowder, covered 12.00-24.00
7½" coupe soup 8.00-15.00
8" serving, round 8.00-12.00
9" serving, round 9.00-15.00
11" salad 15.00-25.00
15" serving, rare .... 35.00-50.00*†
1 pint 8.00-15.00
Butter tray and cover, oblong 20.00-45.00
Candle holders, rare, Moby Dick only ones known 100.00
Casserole, 8" (inside diameter), covered 15.00-45.00
Coffee pots, After Dinner, 2-cup 40.00-65.00
regular, 6-cup 25.00-45.00
Creamers, open, individual 7.00-14.00
open, regular 8.00-12.00
Cups and saucers, After Dinner cup 10.00-18.00
saucer 2.00- 4.00
tea cup 10.00-18.00
saucer 2.00- 6.00
jumbo cup 15.00-25.00
saucer 4.00- 6.00
Jam jar, notched lid 30.00-50.00
Muffin cover only (no matching tray) 35.00-50.00
Mug, 3½", 8 oz., applied handle 15.00-25.00
Pickle, 6" round, tab handle (possibly Kent dinnerware only) . 10.00-15.00
Pitchers, 4½" 1 pint jug, open 12.00-18.00
4½" 1 pint jug, covered 15.00-25.00
2 quart, open 18.00-27.00
2 quart, covered 22.00-32.00
2 quart disk (early), Ultra California only 16.00-30.00
Plates, 6½" bread & butter .... 3.00- 6.00*†
(Salamina only, 20.00)

7½″ salad . . . . 6.00- 9.00*†
(Salamina only, 30.00)
8½″ luncheon (possibly Kent dinnerware only) . . . . 7.00-10.00*†
(Salamina only, 45.00)
9½″ luncheon . . . . 8.00-12.00*†
(Salamina only, 65.00)
10½″ dinner . . . . 9.00-15.00*†
(Salamina only, 75.00)
12″ chop . . . . 12.00-25.00*†
(Salamina only, 95.00)
14″ chop . . . . 15.00-27.00*†
(Salamina only, 150.00)
17″ chop . . . . 25.00-35.00†
(Disney patterns, Our America
or Moby Dick demand five times
the above price.)
(Salamina only, 200.00)
Sauce boat 12.00-25.00
Shakers, salt 5.00-10.00
pepper 5.00-10.00
Sugar bowl, covered, individual 10.00-18.00
covered, regular 7.00-15.00
Teapot, 6-cup 20.00-45.00
Tumbler, 13 oz., iced tea, concave sides 15.00-25.00
Tureenette, 7″, notched cover 35.00-50.00

*For Disney patterns, Kent's Our America and Moby Dick and Blanding's Aquarium,
triple the price for these items.
†The following patterns demand double the price:

Bouquet
Coral Reef
Delight
Ecstasy
Flora
Glamour
Harvest
Hawaiian Flowers
Hilo
Honolulu
Joy
Lei Lani
Vera

Melinda Shape

The Melinda shape was a Royal Hickman design which was an elaborate shape used for English look-alike traditional patterns. It employed a leaf motif embossed on borders of flatware and on bases of bowls, pitchers and teapots, rising in modeled relief from the handles of holloware and having flower-like finials. Some serving pieces were leaf shaped. A round plate has been found with squared off corners, an unusual shape. According to an ad in the 1942 *Crockery and Glass Journal*, "10 different patterns were available, some handpainted, some print and fill, all underglaze." To date 14 patterns, including the solid color Melinda (later called Native California) are known. Hand-tinted patterns are Chintz, Dolores, May Flower, Cosmos, Fruitdale and Southern Rose. Don Blanding's Hawaii (same as Lei Lani design) was also executed on Melinda. Plain print includes Blossom Time and handpainted includes Monterey, Philodendron, Arcadia, Beverly, and Santa Anita. Some designs are identical, pattern name determined by color difference, such as Cosmos and Blossom Time.

Goes to Sea was a personalized handpainted yachting dinnerware on the Melinda shape with either the Philodendron or Monterey colored border and offered through special order. The company brochure described it as "fine dinnerware . . . complete with the name of your yacht, copper etched in rope design and house flag and yacht club burgee on each piece in full color under permanent glaze". It is rare but fortunately one example was available for photographing, the Four Winds cup. Four Winds was designed for the yacht that sailed the Transpacific Yacht Club Race from Los Angeles to Honolulu (year unknown). Sal-Al III, another pattern, has been reported.

This is the solid color Native California. Colors known are dark turquoise, light turquoise, blue, pink, yellow. All have mark 18 unless noted.

Top, left to right:
12½" diameter bowl with footed base, 4½" deep (12); 13½" platter; 9½" plate (20); 8½" rim soup.

Center, left to right:
Salt and pepper shakers (U); demitasse cup and saucer; 7½" plate; creamer.

Bottom, left to right:
5½" fruit; 6½" plate (17, only one in the group with Melinda mark).

Melinda transfer prints are pictured, all have mark 19, exceptions noted.

Top, left to right: Fruitdale 9½″ plate; Chintz 13½″ chop plate; Blossom Time 8″ (inside diameter*) covered casserole (mark 19 without words "handpainted under glaze") -- note the embossed leaf handles and leaves on lid. Center, left to right: Chintz butter tray and cover; Fruitdale 4″ creamer**, Chintz 4″ sugar**; May Flower 7½″ plate (21). Bottom left to right: Chintz 3″ creamer**; Dolores 3″ sugar** (20); Four Winds cup with Monterey trim (marked "Made Especially for Don Carlos Heintz, Skipper of the Four Winds by Vernon Kilns"); Monterey saucer; Dolores 5½″ fruit (20); Southern Rose sauce boat (4 line mark giving pattern name, "handpainted, underglazes, by Vernon Kilns, U.S.A.", in block letters, similar to mark 16).

Handpainted and handtinted patterns on Melinda shape are shown, all have mark 19 exceptions noted.

Top, left to right: Dolores 14″ oval platter; Monterey 1 quart pitcher; Chintz coffee pot. Center, left to right: Arcadia 6 cup teapot; Fruitdale 2-tier server with brass handle; Chintz salt shaker; May Flower pepper shaker (shaker marked only with pattern name and "made in U.S.A."); May Flower 9½″ oval vegetable. Bottom, left to right: Monterey leaf-shaped 12″ relish; Philodendron demitasse cup and saucer (21); Southern Rose 2-part leaf-shaped serving dish (has same mark as sauce boat in previous photo).

*Actual diameter of the casserole is 11″ including handles. Inside diameter is described in company price lists.
**Note two sizes of creamer and sugar.

The following are all known patterns on the Melinda shape.

Name/Number	Description	Approx. Date of Production	Artist
Arcadia	Handpainted brown and mustard laurel wreath border.	1942 Special Order 1950-1955	
Beverly	Handpainted rose blossoms, leaves encircle rims.	1942	
Blossom Time	Allover blossoms, deep blue transfer. Same as Cosmos except for color.	1942	
Chintz	Traditional hand-tinted floral allover transfer. English style.	1942 Special order 1950	
Cosmos	Allover floral transfer, hand-tinted red print. Same as Blossom Time, different color.	1942	
Dolores	Traditional border print, hand-tinted large blossoms. English style.	1942-1947	
Four Winds	Special order personalized yacht pattern, maroon and blue border.	1950	
Fruitdale	Transfer design of array of fruit, brilliantly hand-tinted print. English style.	1942-1947	
Hawaii	Transfer lotus flower, allover handtinted maroon print. Same as Lei Lani, but different shape.	1942	Blanding
May Flower	Transfer, hand-tinted large spray of flowers. English style.	1942-1950, 1953-1955. Special order 1950-1953, 1955.	
Melinda	First name given to Native California. Solid colors. Shape also called Melinda.	1942	Hickman
Monterey	Handpainted leaf border, handles and finials, red and blue colors. Same as Philodendron, different color.	1942 Special order 1950-1954	
Native California	Solid pastel colors: blue, yellow, pink, green and aqua.	1942-1947	Hickman
Philodendron	Handpainted leaf border, handles and finials, green and yellow colors. Same as Monterey, different colors.	1942 Special order 1950-1954	
Sal-Al III	See Four Winds		
Santa Anita	Handpainted border. Pink blossoms connected by brown wavy lines.	1942	
Santa Barbara	Allover transfer pattern, brown print, hand-tinted blue and yellow flowers.	1939	
Santa Maria	Allover transfer pattern, purple print, hand-tinted blue and yellow flowers.	1939	

Santa Paula	Allover transfer pattern, pink print, hand-tinted blue and yellow flowers.	1939
Santa Rosa	Allover transfer pattern, blue print, hand-tinted blue and yellow flowers.	1939
Southern Rose	Transfer, hand-tinted floral bouquet.	1942
Wheat	Transfer, hand-tinted large spray of blossoms and sheaths of wheat. NOTE: This pattern has the Harmony House backstamp, also reading "Exclusively for Sears, Roebuck & Co."	1942

Prices For Melinda

Bowls, 5½" fruit	3.00- 5.00
6" lug chowder	5.00-9.00
8" rim soup	7.00-12.00
9" serving, round	8.00-12.00
10" serving, oval	9.00-12.00
Butter tray and cover, oblong	15.00-35.00
Casserole, covered, 8" (inside diameter)	15.00-35.00
Coffee pot, covered, 8-cup	25.00-35.00
Comport, low, 12½" diameter, scarce	20.00-35.00
Creamer, regular, 3" or 4"	6.00-12.00
Cups and saucers, After Dinner cup	10.00-15.00
saucer	2.00- 4.00
Tea cup	8.00-12.00
saucer	2.00- 3.00
Egg cup	8.00-15.00
Pitchers, 1½ pint	10.00-12.00
1 quart	12.00-15.00
2 quart	15.00-20.00
Plates, 6½" bread and butter	3.00- 6.00
7½" salad	4.00- 8.00
9½" luncheon	6.00-12.00
10½" dinner	8.00-14.00
12" chop	12.00-20.00
14" chop	15.00-25.00
Two-tier	10.00-15.00
Three-tier	12.00-20.00
Platters, 12"	12.00-18.00
14"	15.00-20.00
16"	17.00-30.00
Relish, 11", 2-part	15.00-20.00
12", single	12.00-15.00
14", 4-part leaf shape	35.00-40.00
Sauce boat	12.00-20.00
Shakers, salt	5.00- 8.00
pepper	5.00- 8.00
Sugar, covered	8.00-12.00
Teapot, covered, 6-cup	20.00-35.00

San Fernando Shape

Another elaborate shape (designer not known) is believed to have been introduced during the same period as Melinda. It has no solid color counterpart. The flatware has scalloped rims and the holloware has fluted pedestal styled bases with fancy scrolled handles. The traditional patterns executed on this shape were extremely popular and again offered an English look. The provincial R.F.D. pattern included two different figural salt and pepper shakers (hurricane lamps and mail boxes). There are six known patterns, all are transfer prints. The two plain prints are Early Days and R.F.D. The four hand-tinted prints are Vernon's 1860, Hibiscus, Vernon Rose and Desert Bloom. For R.F.D. and Vernon's 1860, detailed backstamps were specially designed.

Top, left to right: Vernon's 1860 coffee pot and 10½ " plate; Early Days 7½ " plate. Center, left to right: R.F.D. sauce boat with attached underplate; Vernon's 1860 saucer; Early Days after dinner cup and saucer. Bottom, left to right: R.F.D. 10" olive dish; Vernon's 1860 8" rim soup; R.F.D. butter tray and cover.

Vernon's 1860 soup tureen, 13" diameter. Also there is a 15" plate stand to match.

102

Top, left to right: Hibiscus 12″ oval platter; Vernon Rose 14″ chop plate: Hibiscus demitasse cup and saucer; Desert Bloom 10½″ plate. Bottom, left to right: Hibiscus 2-tier server; chowder; salt shaker (U); Desert Bloom salt shaker (U); Hibiscus 10″ oval vegetable; tea cup and saucer; 5½″ fruit.

All items in the previous two photos have mark 21, except for R.F.D., Vernon's 1860 and as noted.

The following are all known patterns on the San Fernando shape.

Name/Number	Description	Approx. Date of Production	Artist
Desert Bloom	Transfer, hand-tinted rust print of tiny floral, wide border. English style.	1944 Special order 1955	
Early Days	Traditional scenes of 1860 surrounded by wide floral border, different scenes decorate. Transfer in allover deep rose print. English style. Same as Vernon's 1860, different color.	1944 Special order 1950-1955	
Hibiscus	Transfer, hand-tinted yellow tiny flowers on brown print. English style.	1944 Special order 1954	
R.F.D.	Brown rooster, green plaid border, provincial transfer.	1953 Special order 1954	
Vernon's 1860	Transfer scenes of 1860 America wide floral border, handtinted brown print.	1944 Special order 1954	Botsford (sometimes signed)
Vernon Rose	Transfer. Single large yellow rose, small blossoms, hand-tinted on cream background.	1944 Special order 1950-1954	

Prices For San Fernando

Bowls, 5½" fruit	3.00- 5.00
5½" salad, individual	6.00-10.00
6" lug chowder	5.00-10.00
8" rim soup	7.00-12.00
9" serving, round	9.00-15.00
10" serving, oval	10.00-17.00
10½" salad	15.00-25.00
*Butter tray and cover, oblong (R.F.D. only)	25.00
Casserole, covered, 8" (inside diameter)	18.00-40.00
*Coaster, 4" (R.F.D. only)	8.00
Coffee pot, covered, 8-cup	30.00-40.00
Creamer, regular	8.00-12.00
Cups and saucers, After Dinner cup	10.00-15.00
saucer	2.00- 5.00
tea cup	10.00-12.00
saucer	2.00- 3.00
Egg cup, double	10.00-15.00
*Mug, 9 oz. (R.F.D. only)	12.00
Olive dish, 10"	12.00-18.00
Plates, 6½" bread and butter	3.00- 6.00
7½" salad	4.00- 8.00
9½" luncheon	6.00-12.00
10½" dinner	8.00-15.00
14" chop	15.00-25.00
Two-tier	10.00-15.00
Three-tier	12.00-22.00
Platters, 12"	12.00-18.00
14"	15.00-20.00
16"	18.00-35.00
Sauce boat with attached plate	20.00-30.00
Shakers, salt	5.00- 8.00
pepper	5.00- 8.00
*figural mail box (R.F.D. only), pair	20.00
*figural lantern (R.F.D. only), pair	20.00
*Spoon holder (R.F.D. only)	15.00
Soup Tureen, covered, 13", notched cover (none for R.F.D.)	50.00-65.00
15" plate stand (none for R.F.D.)	15.00-20.00
Sugar, covered	8.00-15.00
Teapot, covered, 6-cup	25.00-40.00
*Tumbler, 14 oz. (R.F.D. only)	15.00

*These items not shown in company price lists for any San Fernando patterns except R.F.D.

San Marino Shape

San Marino, a mid-1940's shape was a complete departure from the traditional. With streamlined, elongated holloware and coupe flatware, some lines were handpainted. Some had printed designs and some interesting glazes. It was an exciting new look widely accepted by young housewives. The shape continued to be reproduced until the company went out of business. Of known patterns, three are basic solid color lines: Casual California, California Shadows, and California Originals (also called California Heritage). Casual California in solid colors featured new colors described in company catalogs as Lime Green and Dusk Gray. California Originals was in unusual colors of Raisin Purple, Redwood Brown, Almond Yellow and Vineyard Green. Both California Shadows and California Originals have interesting drip glazes. A patent was applied for to cover the method of the drip glaze technique for California Originals (California Heritage). The backstamp for this pattern is a variation of mark 20 with the words "Cerametal-Process, Patent Applied for" added above the pattern name within the scroll.

California Originals, four from a set of five mixing bowls; a complete set is hard to find.

9″ Vineyard Green; 7″ Vineyard Green; 5″ Raisin Purple; and 6″ Almond Yellow. The 8″ Redwood Brown is missing from the set.

All the solid color patterns are pictured and are marked 20, exceptions noted.

Top, left to right:
California Originals Redwood Brown 10 cup coffee server, bakelite handle (20 cerametal variation); California Shadows Cocoa Brown 13½″ oval platter; California Originals Almond Yellow 8 cup teapot measuring 11″ lengthwise (20 cerametal variation).

2nd row, left to right:
Casual California Mahogany Brown 8 cup teapot measuring 14½″ lengthwise; four 14 oz. tumblers, three are Casual California in Dusk Gray (22), Mahogany Brown (22), Pine Green (U), and one California Originals in Raisin Purple (U).

3rd row, left to right:
California Casual Lime Green butter tray and cover; Mocha Brown creamer (20 or 27*); Dawn Pink sugar bowl, California Heritage Almond Yellow 9″ vegetable (20 cerametal variation); Casual California Lime Green 9 oz. mug (22) and Mahogany Brown 9 oz. mug (marked "Made in California" only, block letters).

Bottom, left to right:
Casual California Lime Green 4″ coaster; California Originals Vineyard Green sugar bowl (20 cerametal variation); Casual California Lime Green gourd-shaped salt shaker (U) and ¼ pint pitcher.

A 5½″ fruit dish identical to the San Marino shape has been reported, backstamped "SUNSET POTTERY, MADE IN CALIFORNIA, U.S.A." and pictures the sun on the horizon. It could possibly be a Vernon Kilns product under another name.

*Mocha Brown serving pieces were also combined with the Heyday pattern.

Pictured are patterns found in the San Marino shape, all marked 21 except where noted.

Top, left to right: Mojave* sugar bowl (41); Hawaiian Coral 8 cup teapot; Raffia 5½" fruit; Sun Garden 6½" plate and creamer (46, designer pattern). Center, left to right: Seven Seas 11" platter; Shadow Leaf 10" plate; Barkwood ¼ pint pitcher; Hawaiian Coral 10" plate and double egg cup (U). Bottom, left to right: Raffia cup (U) and saucer; Bel Air butter tray and cover (22); Gayety cup (U) and saucer; Trade Winds creamer (U); Vernonware dealer sign; Hawaiian Coral individual 4" covered casserole (22) and butter pat; Casual California 11" Dawn Pink platter (20); Heyday 6" plate.

Lei Lani is shown as it appears on the San Marino shape.

Creamer; 10" plate; salt shaker.

*Mojave may have been jobber or premium ware since the Vernon Kilns name is not on the backstamp.

The following are all known patterns on the San Marino shape.

Name/Number	Description	Approx. Date of Production	Artist
Barkwood*	Warm brown on beige, hand-painted wood grain effect. Same as Raffia and Shantung except for colors.	1953-1958	
Bel Air	Handpainted green and brown stripes crossing on ivory background. Same as Gayety except for color.	Late 1940 Special order 1955	
California Originals (also called California Heritage)	Drip glaze border in solid colors: Almond Yellow, Raisin Purple, Redwood Brown, Vineyard Green.	1947 Special order 1954	
California Shadows	Solid color, streaked drip glaze border, mottled effect on lids. 1953 Cocoa Brown and Antique Gray, 1954 Cocoa Brown only.	1953 Special order 1955	
Casual California	Solid colors: 1950 Acacia Yellow, Lime Green, Mahogany Brown, Pine Green; 1953 added Dawn Pink, Dusk Gray, Snowhite; 1954 discontinued Mahogany Brown, Snowhite, added Mocha Brown, Turquoise Blue; 1955 colors were Dawn Pink, Dusk Gray, Mocha Brown, Turquoise Blue.	1947-1956 Special order 1956	
Gayety	Handpainted stripes in soft green and rose on ivory. Same as Bel Air, different color.	1948 Special order 1954	
Hawaiian Coral	Border in spattered blend of colors brown, yellow and green on cream background.	1952 Special order 1956	
Heyday*	Geometric interlocking circles in deep green and brown, spattered beige background, mocha serving pieces.	1954-1958	
Lei Lani (1947-1955)	Transfer, allover hand-tinted maroon print. (Hawaii is the same pattern only on the Melinda shape.)	1947 Special order 1954-1955	Blanding
Mojave	Handpainted bands of yellow, dark green, brown on rim. (Unmarked V.K.)	1955	
Raffia	Handpainted texture pattern, to resemble fiber. Henna on green background. Same as Shantung and Barkwood except for color.	1953-1954	
Seven Seas	Stylized sail boats, brown and blue colors on ivory background.	1954	
Shadow Leaf	Stylized red and green floral on greentone swirl background. Same as Trade Winds, different colors.	1954-1955 Special order 1956	

Name/Number	Description	Approx. Date of Production	Artist
Shantung	Handpainted texture pattern to resemble cloth. Dark brown on bright green background. Same as Barkwood and Raffia except for color.	1953	
Sun Garden	Butterflies and flowers transfer, hand-tinted on pale green background.	1953	Jean Ames
Trade Winds	Rust and chartreuse floral on neutral swirl background. Same as Shadow Leaf except for color.	1954-1955 Special order 1956	
778	Evenly spaced red splashes on rim, white background. Perhaps restaurant ware.	1950	

*Metlox continued pattern for a short time.

Prices For San Marino

Ash Tray, 4″ (coaster) 4.00- 6.00
   5½″ round 6.00- 9.00
Bowls, 5½″ fruit 3.00- 5.00
  *5½″ salad, individual 6.00-10.00
  6″ chowder 5.00- 9.00
  7½″ serving, round 6.00- 9.00
  8½″ coupe soup 6.00-10.00
  9″ serving, round 7.00-10.00
  10″ divided serving, double 8.00-15.00
  *10½″ salad 10.00-20.00
Mixing bowls, nest of 4
  nest of 5
    5″ 4.00- 6.00
    6″ 5.00- 7.00
    7″ 6.00- 9.00
    8″ 7.00-11.00
    9″ 8.00-13.00
*Butter pat, individual, 2½″ (Barkwood, Belair, Gayety and
  Hawaiian Coral)..................................... 5.00- 8.00
Butter tray and cover, oblong 12.00-30.00
Casserole, covered, 8″ (inside diameter) 12.00-35.00
  *covered, 4″, individual 12.00-18.00
  *covered, 4″ chicken pie, individual, stick handle 12.00-18.00
*"Casserole Hot", metal stand with candle warmer 12.00
*"Casserole Round-Up", metal stand with candle warmer 20.00
Coaster, 4″... 4.00- 6.00
Coffee Server & stopper, 10-cup 14.00-20.00
  Stopper only 4.00- 8.00
*Coffee Hot", metal stand with candle warmer 12.00
Creamer, regular 6.00- 9.00
Cups and saucers, tea cup............................. 7.00-10.00
  saucer.. 2.00- 3.00

*Jumbo cup	10.00-15.00
saucer	3.00- 5.00
*Colossal cup	25.00-45.00
saucer	10.00-15.00
*Custard, 3″, rare	12.00-20.00
*Egg cup, double	10.00-12.00
Flower pot, *3″	8.00-12.00
saucer	4.00- 5.00
*4″	10.00-15.00
saucer	5.00- 7.00
*5″	12.00-20.00
saucer	6.00- 8.00
Mug, 9 oz.	8.00-15.00
Pitchers, *¼ pint	5.00- 8.00
*½ pint	6.00-10.00
1 pint	8.00-12.00
1 quart	12.00-20.00
2 quart	15.00-25.00
*Syrup drip-cut top	25.00-45.00
Plates, *2½″ lapel plate with pin (Barkwood, Bel Air, Gayety and Hawaiian Coral	15.00-18.00
6″ bread and butter	2.00- 4.00
7½″ salad	3.00- 6.00
10″ dinner	6.00-12.00
13″ chop	12.00-20.00
Two-tier	10.00-18.00
Three-tier	12.00-20.00
Platters, 9½″	7.00-10.00
11″	8.00-15.00
13½″	12.00-20.00
Sauce boat	10.00-15.00
Shakers, salt, gourd	3.00- 6.00
pepper, gourd	3.00- 6.00
*salt, large (Montecito shape)	5.00- 8.00
*pepper mill (Montecito shape)	15.00-30.00
*Spoon holder	10.00-15.00
Sugar, covered	6.00-12.00
Teapot, covered, 8-cup, 11″ long	18.00-30.00
14½″ long	25.00-45.00
Tumbler, convex sides, 14 oz.	10.00-18.00

*Made briefly 1953-1956.

Lotus Shape and Variation

In lieu of the company name for the shape, the Lotus pattern name was chosen to identify a shape utilized for three separate patterns. Coupe plates with offset rims and holloware having a bulky look characterize this line. The individual patterns were interesting and colorful. They were Lotus, Chinling, and Vintage. A complete set in lime green has been reported. The patterns were introduced in 1950 and were short-lived. A variation was Pan American Lei which combined the San Marino flatware with the Lotus shaped holloware.

Examples of the Lotus line, all have mark 21.

Top, left to right: Chinling 10½″ plate (note offset rim); Lotus sugar bowl. Bottom, left to right: Vintage teapot (lid missing); Lotus creamer; Chinling sugar bowl.

Pan American Lei pattern was designed to coordinate with Heisey etched stemware pattern #518. The promotion was sponsored by Pan American Air Lines. The premiere showing was in Honolulu on June 26, 1950 and the American mainland premiere was in 1950. The pattern has a designer backstamp #44. A former employee believed Blanding designed this pattern, but it is not signed in the usual way.

Top, left to right: 9 oz. mug; 10″ plate; teapot. Bottom, left to right: 8″ covered vegetable (13″ diameter including handles); 5½″ fruit; tea cup and saucer; salt and pepper shakers.

The following are all known patterns on the Lotus shape.

Name/Number	Description	Approx. Date of Production
Chinling	Floral spray in Oriental style, ivory. background.	1950
Lotus	Large red and yellow lotus flower, buds and leaf, ivory background.	1950
Pan American Lei	(Lotus variation). Transfer. Hand-tinted flower lei design on pink background.	1950
Vintage	Bunch of purple grapes, brown leaves and tendrils on ivory background.	1950

Prices For Lotus and Pan American Lei

	Lotus	Pan American
Ash Tray		7.50
Butter tray and cover, oblong	20.00	30.00
Bowls, 5½″ fruit	4.00	5.00
6″ chowder	7.00	9.00
8½″ soup, coupe		10.00
9″ serving, round	12.00	15.00
10½″ salad		20.00
12½″ salad	18.00	
serving, divided, double	12.00	15.00
Coffee or teapot, covered, 8-cup	25.00	30.00
Casserole, covered, 8″ (inside diameter)	25.00	35.00
Creamer	10.00	12.00
Cups, tea	8.00	10.00
saucer	2.00	3.00
Mug, 9 oz.	12.00	15.00
Pitcher, 2 qt. jug	18.00	22.00
Plates, 6″ coupe		4.00
6½″ offset	4.00	
7½″ coupe		6.00
7½″ offset	6.00	
10″ coupe		10.00
10½″ offset	10.00	
13″ chop	18.00	20.00
Platter, 13½″ coupe		20.00
14″ offset	18.00	

Sauce boat.	15.00	18.00
Shakers, salt	6.00	7.00
salt cellar (large Montecito shape)		8.00
pepper	6.00	7.00
pepper mill (large Montecito, metal fitting for Pan American only)		30.00
Sugar, covered.	12.00	13.00
Tumbler, convex sides, 14 oz.	15.00	16.00

Chatelaine Shape

Chatelaine was a designer shape and pattern by Sharon Merrill in 1953. It was a beautiful dinnerware line that did not sell well due to the impracticality of the shape. Square shaped with embossed leaf corners, leaf handles and finials, it was produced in four solid colors: Bronze and Topaz (undecorated), Jade (leaf subtly decorated) and Platinum (cream colored and leaf boldly decorated). Platinum has been found but was not available for photographing. Mark 47 illustrates how the dinnerware was marked, although not every piece will be marked. There may be slight mark variations, that is, instead of script, "Vernonware, California" (Mark 47), the Vernon Kilns trademark (22) will be stamped and appears in combination with the incised "Chatelaine, a Sharon Merrill Design".

Pictured is an array of Chatelaine.

In Bronze are 16″ platter, creamer, teacup and saucer, salt and pepper shakers. In Topaz, sugar bowl, tea cup and saucer, and in Jade, tea cup and saucer, chowders, 14″ chop plate and 10½″ plates, one standing, the rest stacked.

The following are all known patterns on the Chatelaine shape.

Name/Number	Description	Approx. Date of Production	Artist
Chatelaine	Solid colors Bronze and Topaz. Decorated solid colors Jade and Platinum.	1953	Sharon Merrill

Prices For Chatelaine

	Topaz & Bronze	Platinum & Jade
Bowls, 6" chowder	10.00	12.00
12" salad	25.00	30.00
Cups and saucers, Tea, pedestal	12.00	15.00
Saucer	3.00	3.00
Coffee, flat base	10.00	12.00
Saucer	2.00	3.00
Creamer	15.00	17.00
Plates, 6½" bread and butter	5.00	7.00
7½" salad	8.00	10.00
10½" dinner	12.00	15.00
14" chop	25.00	30.00
Platter, 16"	30.00	35.00
Shakers, salt	7.00	8.00
pepper	7.00	8.00
Sugar, covered	20.00	22.00
Teapot, covered	35.00	45.00

Anytime Shape
    Since the company name for this shape is not known, the pattern name "Anytime" has been adopted for identification. The shape, designed by Elliott House, Art director at the time -- according to Doug Bothwell -- was introduced about 1955. Flatware is coupe shaped and holloware somewhat barrel shaped with ring handles and finials. Patterns are simple with at least four having solid color companion serving pieces that accent the color in the pattern. Most have peppered backgrounds. The nine known patterns in this shape are Tickled Pink and Heavenly Days (identical design except for colors), Anytime, Imperial, Sherwood, Frolic, Young in Heart, Rose-A-Day*, Dis 'N Dot. Not all patterns were available for photos.

Top, left to right: Heavenly Days 7½" plate (27); Anytime 10" plate (25) and 2 quart 10" pitcher (23); Lollipop Tree (*Not* Anytime shape, but Year 'Round) 1 pint batter bowl (27). Center, left to right: Tickled Pink butter tray and cover (23) and companion solid color pepper and salt shakers with wood tops (U); Heavenly Days aqua 9" vegetable bowl (23); Tickled Pink pink 6" chowder (U) and gravy boat; Rose-A-Day* 3 part relish (27). Bottom, left to right: Tickled Pink sugar and pink lid (24); butter pat (became a lapel pin when fitted with pin on back); creamer (24); pink tea cup (U); saucer (24); mug (27).

*Rose-A-Day dinnerware was featured in a patio scene during a teenage party in the movie, *Summer Love*, starring Jill St. John in 1956.

Top, left to right: Imperial 10" plate (48) -- a designer pattern, "Show Stopper", the graffito design was carved with a penknife under the glaze. According to Doug Bothwell, former employee, the production people did not like the pattern since the color contaminated the kilns, so it was discontinued after a short time; Sherwood 13½" platter (26). Bottom, left to right: Sherwood 10" brass handled server (25); 5½" fruit (27); 14 oz. tumbler (23); Seven Seas platter (belongs in the San Marino group though pictured here).

The following are all known patterns on the Anytime shape.

Name/Number	Description	Approx. Date of Production
Anytime*	Abstract vertical bands of yellow, mocha, gray; cream peppered background, mint green serving pieces, lids.	1955-1958
Dis 'N Dot	Abstract offcenter vertical lines and dots in blue, green, and mustard on ivory.	1957-1958
Frolic	Abstract floral, gold, purple and aqua on ivory peppered background.	1955
Heavenly Days*	Geometric design of small squares and crosses in aqua, pink and mocha-charcoal. Solid aqua cups and serving pieces. Same as Tickled Pink in other colors.	1956-1958
Imperial	Sgraffito abstract in white lines on ebony background, shaded swirl to soft gray center.	1955-1956
Rose-A-Day*	Single pink rose, scattered leaves in soft colors. Satin ivory background.	1956-1958
Sherwood*	Leaves scattered in colors of gold, bronze, and brown on beige peppered background.	1955-1958
Tickled Pink*	Geometric design·of small squares and crosses in pink and charcoal. Solid pink cups and serving pieces. Same as Heavenly Days, except for color.	1955-1958

*Metlox continued pattern for a short time.

Prices for Anytime listed with Year 'Round.

Year 'Round Shape

This was one of the last shapes designed by Vernon Kilns, and again a pattern name has been adopted to identify the shape because the company name is unknown. Only two patterns in this group were available for pictures. One is the Lollipop Tree batter bowl, the other is the Blueberry Hill platter on the following page. The shape is similar to the Anytime shape, but platters and vegetable bowls are rectangular instead of oval, finials are button shaped, creamers and salt shakers are tall and slender, sugar bowls are short and pepper shakers are ball-shaped with slender necks. Teapots and coffee pots have pottery stands. Some patterns have a satin finish, while others have peppered backgrounds. Known patterns are Year 'Round, Lollipop Tree, Blueberry Hill, Country Cousin and Young in Heart.

Here are drawings of the Year 'Round shape.

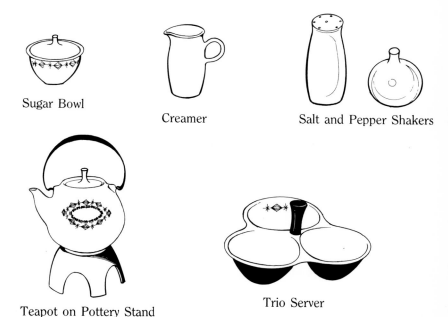

Sugar Bowl

Creamer

Salt and Pepper Shakers

Teapot on Pottery Stand

Trio Server

In 1953, Table Accessories were added to complement the San Marino and Montecito lines. These are black wrought-iron holders complete with glass candle warmers for "Coffee Hot", "Casserole Hot", and "Casserole Round-Up". The Round-Up was designed to hold a covered casserole and six 4″ individual casseroles or chicken pies. All are illustrated in the drawing below.

Metal stands, believed to be brass, with candlewarmers were made for the Anytime shape and were called "Casserole Hot", "Gravy Hot", and "Coffee Hot". The stands were similar to the black wrought-iron server-warmers. Pottery self-stands were made for the Year 'Round line to hold the casserole, coffee pot, gravy boat and teapot.

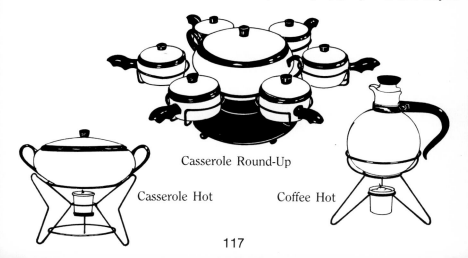

Casserole Round-Up

Casserole Hot

Coffee Hot

The following are all known patterns on the Year 'Round shape.

Name/Number	Description	Approx. Date of Production	Artist
Blueberry Hill	Abstract pale blue floral, brown leaves, satin ivory background.	1957-1958	
Country Cousin	Geometric border of squares and diamonds framing florals and people. Modern provincial, mustard on ivory.	1957-1958	
Lollipop Tree	Abstract lollipops, softly colored, satin ivory background.	1957-1958	
Year 'Round	Geometric circle design in yellow, mocha and gray on creamy white background. Serving pieces, lids and stands in mocha.	1957-1958	
Young in Heart	Dainty scattered florals, subtle yellow, aqua, charcoal and mocha colors on cream peppered background.	1956-1958	

Prices For Anytime and Year 'Round

Bowls, 5½" fruit	3.00- 4.00
6" chowder	4.00- 6.00
7½" serving, round (Anytime)	4.00- 6.00
9" serving, round	5.00- 8.00
9½" serving, divided	6.00- 9.00
one pint, handled bowl (Year 'Round)	5.00- 8.00
soup, coupe (Anytime)	5.00- 8.00
Butter pat, 2½", individual (Tickled Pink, 1955)	3.00- 5.00
Butter tray and cover, oblong	12.00-18.00
Casserole, covered, 8" (inside diameter)	12.00-18.00
"Casserole Hot", metal stand (Anytime)	7.00
pottery stand (Year 'Round)	10.00
Coffee pot, covered, 6-cup (Year 'Round)	12.00-18.00
8-cup (Anytime)	12.00-18.00
"Coffee Hot", metal stand (Anytime)	7.00
pottery stand (Year 'Round)	10.00
Creamer	6.00- 8.00
Cup and saucer, tea	5.00- 8.00
Gravy boat	5.00- 8.00
"Gravy Hot", metal stand (Anytime)	7.00
pottery stand (Year 'Round)	10.00
Mug, 12 oz.	8.00-12.00
Pitchers, 1 pint (Anytime)	7.00-10.00
1 quart	8.00-12.00
2 quart, 10" (Anytime)	10.00-15.00

Plates, *Lapel plate with pin, 2½″ (Tickled Pink, 1955) ..... | 12.00
6″ bread and butter .... | 2.00- 4.00
7½″ salad .... | 3.00- 5.00
10″ dinner................................ | 5.00- 8.00
13″ chop (Anytime) .... | 9.00-12.00
Two-tier (Anytime) .... | 10.00-12.00
Three-tier (Anytime) .... | 12.00-15.00
Platters, 9½″ (Anytime)................ | 7.00- 9.00
11″ .... | 8.00-10.00
13½″ .... | 9.00-12.00
Relish, 3-section (Anytime) .... | 7.00-10.00
Shakers, salt........................ | 3.00- 5.00
pepper .... | 3.00- 5.00
Sugar, covered .... | 8.00-10.00
Teapot, covered .... | 15.00-20.00
"Tea Hot", pottery stand (Year 'Round)............ | 12.00
Trio Buffet Server (Year 'Round) .... | 8.00-12.00
Tumbler, 14 oz. (Anytime), convex .... | 12.00

These pieces were found too late to be photographed with their separate groups.

Top, left to right: 778, 9½″ plate (San Marino, 19); Bennison Ring No. 3, 10″ lavender bowl. Bottom, left to right: Cosmos 10½″ plate (Melinda, 19); North Wind (appears to be Montecito, 21); jumbo cup and saucer, unknown pattern (Ultra, U); Blueberry Hill 13½″ platter (Year 'Round, 27); chowder bowl, pattern unknown (Montecito, marked only "Handpainted Underglaze Pottery").

THE LAST YEARS

After World War II, the United States government encouraged trade with countries whose economies had suffered during the war. Consequently, our country was flooded with imports from Japan, England and Scandinavia.

To offset this competition, an efficient sales department was organized with agents in Alaska, Hawaii, South America, Canadian provinces of British Columbia and Ontario and all major cities in the United States. Doug Bothwell, son-in-law of Faye Bennison, was persuaded to join Vernon Kilns as Vice President in Charge of Sales in 1952. Major sales campaigns were conducted by Zepha Bogert and her husband, E.V. Bogert, who were the advertising agents for Vernon Kilns. One of their most successful promotionals was the "Vernon Girls", a group of young ladies who arranged table displays in major department stores all over the country. Each girl was fictitiously known as "Ruth Vernon". Orders poured in from this campaign.

Other sales aids were developed by the Bogerts and made available to stores. The ceramic dealer sign pictured in dinnerware photos was designed especially to hold price cards for "Starter sets". Other sales aids available were brochures or price cards for display on store counters or shelves, a sales training 78 rpm record, at $1.50 postpaid recorded by "Ruth Vernon", television slides and copy to provide stores with interesting television spots, a 16mm motion picture *A Date with a Vernon Dish* in full color with sound track available in 20 or 30 minute lengths for schools, clubs, churches and department store promotions (featured table settings and a trip through the factory), and a series of 35mm slides along with a 20-minute speech available to anyone wanting to give a talk.

In 1955 Mr. Bennison retired as President to become Chairman of the Board and was succeeded by Edward Fischer. With Mr. Bennison no longer active, much of the old spirit was gone. Finally, because of the foreign competition and labor costs becoming increasingly burdensom, and in spite of the successful sales campaigns, the unexpected decision to close the business was announced in January 1958. It was a shock and sad day for the many faithful employees, some of whom had been with the company since its inception. In Mr. Bennison's words, "I was heartbroken to close the plant, a wonderful skilled loyal bunch of people who had worked with us." It took most of the year to wind up manufacturing operations. Some surplus pottery was sold to pottery yards.*

Manufacturing totally ceased and the company disbanded in 1958 and Faye Bennison and Edward Fischer remained the active principals of the corporation until 1969 when Vernon Kilns was finally legally dissolved. Faye Bennison passed away five years later on August 31, 1974 at age 91.

Because of ever-growing collector interest, Vernon Kilns has taken its rightful place as a major contributor to American pottery history.

*Metlox Potteries of Manhattan Beach, California bought the molds and modifying some shapes continued producing some patterns: Brown Eyed Susan, Organdie, Sherwood, Anytime, Tickled Pink and Barkwood for at least a year (possibly a few other patterns too). During the transition, Metlox continued use of Vernon Kilns last Vernonware backstamps but their items were additionally marked "by Metlox", according to Doug Bothwell who transferred to Metlox as head of the Vernonware Division.